MINDFULNESS
FOR THE ULTIMATE ATHLETE

Mastering the Balance
Between *Power* and *Peace*

Prince Daniels Jr.

Mindfulness for the Ultimate Athlete
Copyright © 2020 by Prince Daniels Jr.

www.princedanielsjr.com

Printed in the United States of America

Cover Collage Illustration by Karen Dahlquist, HappyFish Design,
  www.happyfishdesign.com
Cover Design by Siori Kitajima for TheSagerGroup.net
Edited by The Artful Editor, www.artfuleditor.com
Interior Layout by Carla Green, Clarity Designworks,
  www.claritydesignworks.com
Illustrations by Liza Biggers, www.lizabiggers.com

Paperback ISBN 978-1-7352852-1-4
Ebook ISBN 978-1-7352852-0-7

This book is dedicated to the inner God that dwells in every living being in the world. May the words LOVE and GRATITUDE heal us. Peace

CONTENTS

PEACE

PREFACE

The most important thing is to try and inspire people so that they can be great in whatever they want to do.
—KOBE BRYANT

The intentions shared in this book cannot be easily expressed; words are inadequate to describe the true essence of what I want to convey. But if you read these pages with an open mind and an open heart, insights will appear in their purest and most truthful form.

The primary focus of this book is to teach both aspiring and experienced professional athletes how to cultivate their body, mind and spirit into a high level of maturity that leads to achieving a state called "the zone" in which you are functioning as an integrated whole. While exercise, skill training, and nutrition are all important, reaching and sustaining an experience of the zone can only be achieved through the practice of mindfulness and meditation. When these techniques are applied diligently and in a disciplined way, they will take you where you want to go, helping you to access your natural ability to blossom and flourish and manifest your biggest dreams. Why take your game to the next level when you can take it to the highest level? The ultimate level?

This book provides invaluable tools and instructions that some of the world's best athletes have utilized to fuel their success. To follow in their footsteps—or even surpass them—you will need to remember two important things:

First, knowledge acquired is dead without application. Period. You will not become the ultimate athlete just by reading a book. You will not become the ultimate athlete by simply repeating a mantra and expecting something miraculous to occur. Faith without works—without action—will not take you where you want to go. Do the work for the work's sake. Don't look for the rewards, but do envision the outcome. The rewards will be a natural by-product of your effort.

Second, remember this sequence for efficient meditation: Always, always relax the body first, then relax the mind. Once the body and mind connect harmoniously in relaxation, an opening to the spirit naturally occurs, and you will then be able to have a fruitful meditation session.

One more thing: Before immersing yourself in this book, remember to practice good habits such as eating right, reading inspirational material, getting proper sleep, taking care of your body, and cultivating a healthy relationship with yourself. These form the bedrock of a wholesome life and will accelerate the results of your practice.

To align yourself with the ultimate path, contemplate and absorb this simple and practical concept:

When you plant an apple seed in the ground, after some time that apple seed will grow to become an apple tree. Not an orange tree or a banana tree. This is the universal law.

In short, know that you are unique—there is no one quite like you. Practicing good habits is like planting good seeds: Inevitably, good outcomes will germinate and blossom, reflecting and supporting your unique self.

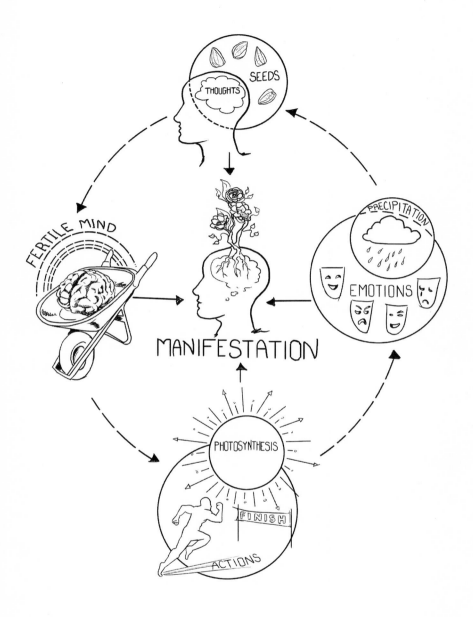

FOREWORD

It's hard to put into words the sensation of being in the zone. On one hand, you feel you have control, like a martial artist or Neo in *The Matrix*. On the other, you're at peace, as if on a busy New York City street but there's only your own thoughts to be heard. Now I don't mean you're in your zone listening to your headphones as you go your merry way. I'm referring to a focus that filters out the current noise and distractions of everyday life and that is laser-focused on the objective at hand. Finding that focus is difficult if there is no vision.

If you cannot envision the best version of yourself, what do you have to work toward? I 100 percent agree with Prince in this book when he says, and I summarize, the spirit is the initial spark giving the vision. Then the mind formulates a plan to get there, your mission if you accept. Lastly, the mind tells the body to act out this vision, creating a perfectly integrated system, spirit, mind, and body capable of overcoming any obstacle.

More important than finding the zone itself is the process. As a former athlete and in my time thus far on this earth, I can attest to the fact that being diligent in the process of becoming that best version of self requires patience—it's not instant coffee. It requires perseverance for when you're brought to your knees but more importantly requires a blueprint so when you're down you're still affixed on the goal you've set for yourself.

I try to operate myself as a business day by day, with one main principle: practicing perfecting any task undertaken. I know I'm not perfect, but giving a perfect effort is nothing more than a mindset.

My father used to tell me that if you're going to do something, do it right. Simply put, how do we know how well we can do anything if we don't give our best attitude and effort?

This leads me back to my goal of being one of the best receivers to play the game. A good friend of mine, Derrick Moore, or "Dmo," taught me the power of meditation throughout college and even early in my NFL career. After severely frustrating seasons to begin my career, the losing began taking its toll. It was recommended I meditate, just spend time five minutes a day in silence, allowing all my issues, distractions, and priorities to fall by the wayside. Over time that five minutes turned into fifteen, twenty minutes, and so on, as I began to armor myself via meditation so that the daily distractions merely became speed bumps on the way to the best version of myself.

It starts with that spark the spirit ignites and that the mind then sets forth as a mission, in turn telling the body to move. For a good business to operate well, it must keep up with what's going in and out of the company, operating expenses, net profits, etc. In turn, that company can now gauge performance based off past performance or basic requirements. Similarly, the body must be conscious of what's going on if it wants to operate to its potential.

I remember the days I'd visualize myself making a great play only for those visions to come to fruition. I couldn't understand why at first, and it seemed so surreal, but the more it happened, the more I realized this zone I continuously fell into was a direct reflection of the efforts committed up to that point in time. It's the perfect practice, the repetition, the great attitude and effort that allow you to be the best version of yourself.

Through our actions we can begin to be our best by focusing our thoughts through meditation, embracing failures and using them as stepping stones, knowing that when you add Spirit to the equation of hard work and effort, you might just get something supernatural. To all who are trying to find the zone, start by stacking good days of work on top of good days and watch how one day those efforts are repaid. Remember, it's a process.

—Calvin "Megatron" Johnson Jr.

INTRODUCTION

I was five years old, living in family housing on the campus of the University of Southern Mississippi. It was Christmas Eve, and like most kids, I was excited because Santa Claus was coming and that meant presents. But we didn't have a chimney, and I was worried. "How is Santa gonna get in?" I asked my parents. "Will he come through the front door?" They assured me that he'd find a way and told me to go to sleep.

During the night I got up to use the bathroom and couldn't help walking down our long hallway to peek around the corner and into the living room. And there it was: a snazzy new BMX bicycle just my height with a bow on top. I hurried back and went to sleep, thrilled to be getting a new bike. Later that same night, I had a dream of riding that bike. It felt like riding on clouds, such a euphoric experience, and so real it felt like it was actually happening.

The next morning, I woke up with a mission, focusing only on that bike. Then I saw the training wheels. I ran to my mom and said, "Ma, last night I had a dream that I can ride my bike without training wheels. I really want to do that!"

She scoffed. "You've never even ridden a bike. You don't know how."

"I know, I know," I said excitedly, "but I did it in my dreams. I rode my bike without training wheels. Can we take them off?"

"You'll have to ask your dad."

And so I did. He was my stepdad, but I thought of him as my real father because he was always positive and honest with me. He taught me good morals and values and was there when I needed him. I will always be grateful for his influence on my life.

"If you think you can ride your bike without training wheels," he said, "then let's go!"

So I got my helmet, went outside, and watched him take off the training wheels. I started getting on the bike, but I was pretty short—my toes were just touching the ground. So I used the curb to help me get up. And then I immediately toppled over. I felt hot inside, and my eyes watered. I was embarrassed—but not for long. As my dad stood there patiently, ready to help if I needed it, I got up and tried again, and fell over again, but I was more prepared this time. It still felt bad, and I held back tears, but then I looked across the street and saw the curb on the other side of the road. It was taller. I walked over with my bike, hoisted myself up, put my foot on the pedal, and pressed down. Then I did so with the other leg with some extra force, and off I went, holding onto the handlebars, gaining control, pedaling, and balancing. And for a moment, everything kind of disappeared because I was in a pure state of bliss, riding and riding and riding. And then *boom!* I crashed into a green trash can. I didn't see *that* in my dream! But I jumped up in jubilation, ecstatic that my dream had become a reality.

This experience had a profound effect on me. I became convinced that each of us has an innate ability to accomplish whatever we can visualize and believe in; a sense of possibility and potential ignites the process of manifesting what we want. As time went on, I had similar experiences that I understood as representing the zone— the best version of you at any point in time. In order to get there, you need to connect with what I call your "Inner-G," or your inner genius—the unique energy that defines who you are at the deepest level.

This is not an easy thing to do. It takes commitment and focus and a belief in your potential. You don't have to be the best in the world at something to be ultimate; you only have to be the best version of yourself, both as an athlete and as a person. The image of a samurai warrior is a good example of what I'm trying to convey.

The samurai began as members of the Japanese military in the twelfth century. Their primary role was protection, not aggression. In addition to their superior skills as swordsmen, they cultivated discipline, balance, mental concentration, and a focus on the present moment—each one a quality of inner strength that defines an ultimate athlete.

Some of my inspiration for this book came from George Leonard, whom I consider a modern-day samurai. He was a unique individual, both an ultimate athlete (a fifth-degree blackbelt in aikido) and one of the founders of the human potential movement of the 1970s. He emphasized the importance of balancing our mental and physical abilities and wrote a number of books about this connection. In one of them, he said, "The athlete that dwells in each of us is more than an abstract ideal. It is a living presence that can change the way we feel and live . . . [It is] the ideal unity of physical and spiritual."[1]

This unity is what the practice of mindfulness and meditation can bring to athletes. They are powerful tools for helping us get out of our own way, overcoming all the noise and programming that keep us from our goals. The idea that such a practice can help athletes improve their mental, emotional, and spiritual fitness isn't new—numerous studies have been done on their benefits to people in all walks of life—but connecting these improvements to enhanced athletic performance is a recent discovery. Much of that research will be presented throughout this book.

> The athlete that dwells in each of us is more than an abstract ideal. It is a living presence that can change the way we feel and live . . . [It is] the ideal unity of physical and spiritual.

How This Book Is Structured

Mindfulness for the Ultimate Athlete is divided into two main sections: Power and Peace. Power refers to the tangible, and Peace to the intangible. Both of them are present in the core of the ultimate athlete, and both need to be in balance. If you try to power your way through everything, you will encounter destruction. If you are too peaceful, there's a danger of passivity and submissiveness.

Power, for me, is about action and includes both the body and the mind. In school and in sports, we learned that power is considered a strength, not a weakness. Someone with power usually comes out ahead. They command respect. And so physical power, used wisely, is good.

The power of the mind is also respected. Mental strength is experienced as having knowledge and information about a subject or a situation and also as the ability to control one's thoughts and emotions. We don't know quite as much about the mind as we do about the body when it comes to athletic performance, but evidence of its impact continues to grow.

Peace is about stillness, and it's more mysterious than Power. In this book I look at peace and the role it plays in the life of the ultimate athlete through the lenses of the spirit and the zone. Its essence is intangible, but when you have those experiences, when your spirit moves you or when everything just seems to click, you know it. We don't have the same knowledge or insights about these intangible forces as we do about the body, or even the mind, but they are equally powerful, perhaps more so.

But the two need to be balanced and their use put to good ends. As with any polarities—hot and cold, up and down, east and west, ebb and flow—Power and Peace make up a whole. Both are necessary. Together they form a single unit, a complete and indivisible whole. When your body, mind, and spirit align, the zone is in reach, which is where Power and Peace come together. The more you learn about them and act on that knowledge, the more empowered you become to accomplish the goals you set for yourself. Each of those four components is briefly described below.

The Body

During my career as a professional football player, fitness was always defined in terms of physical development, outer appearance, and performance. This archaic way of thinking helped me reach a pinnacle of strength and endurance, but on the inside, I felt weak and unfulfilled, as if there was another level I couldn't reach, other muscles and potential I hadn't tapped into. For example, I was convinced that I could run faster and did everything I could to make that so. My mind fixated on factoring in and processing all the equations of speed, trying to connect the dots between what my spirit was convinced I could do and my body actually doing it. *Run faster!* became my mantra, and if I didn't, I felt like a failure.

I then discovered that true fitness is composed of three interlocking parts: the mind, the body, and the spirit. Taking care of your body through nutrition and proper rest is still a priority, but your body is affected by your thoughts, emotions, and the overall quality of your energy, which influences those thoughts and emotions. I realized that my obsession with physical improvement while tuning out my mind and spirit was starting to work against me. I was feeling disconnected. Only when I started to focus on strengthening my mind and my spirit did I begin to unlock my physical potential. The ultimate athlete learns that true power comes only when they've achieved a balance of inner peace and external performance.

The Mind

By using meditation to hone the power of your mind and drawing on the peace that comes when you feel spiritually whole, you can convert energy into matter and turn your dreams into reality. Your mind is the bridge between your spirit, brain, and body. Said another way, what you focus on and energize with your emotions you bring into being, so you want that focus to be clear and those emotions to be healthy. When you take time for deep contemplation, when you exercise consistently and mindfully, you will build more mental strength, increase brain function, lift your mood, and attain better health, which will translate to continual improvements in your chosen sport. The mind is a gym, and meditation is the workout that will unleash your inner and outer potential.

> The mind is a gym, and meditation is the workout that will unleash your inner and outer potential.

The Spirit

The third pillar of true fitness is spiritual fitness. Through the practice of meditation, we can increase our awareness, courage, focus, concentration, and inner tranquility. As we become more in tune with our spiritual self, we become more attuned to who we are and what we're supposed to do in this life. As an athlete aspiring to "ultimate," you will put yourself under tremendous pressure. Things will get hard. There will be dark moments. You will have to dig a bit deeper to see beyond. The way to get through it is to be spiritually rooted, connected with your inner source of inspiration, motivation, and belief. When you are in touch with your inner spirit, your inner fire, you can get through anything.

Ultimate also means excellence not just in how you perform but in who you are—to be and do your best both in and out of the arena of competition. Once professional football was no longer a significant part of my life, I went through a period when I didn't know how to cope. It was difficult for my mind to break its routines and habits, to set new goals and find my identity. I deepened my practice of meditation and realized that my spiritual being was directly connected to my physical experience. As I began to understand myself more deeply through this interconnectedness, I began putting the pieces together again. Magnetizing, empathizing, and communicating with like-spirited people took me to a whole new level of purpose and self-confidence.

To live a wholesome and successful life, you first have to learn about yourself. When you do, you'll be able to understand others because, in the end, we're all the same on the inside. Access to your true spirit, to inner clarity and insight, comes from the practice of mindfulness and the quietness of meditation.

The Zone

When all three pillars of fitness have been developed, you are ready to enter the zone. For me, the zone occurs when I experience my best self. Some have described it as a kind of flow state in which the awareness of time seems to stop and everything is perfectly coordinated. You feel locked in. There is only the present moment and effortless action. It's a space of enhanced confidence and focus where the entire self—body, mind and spirit—is operating as a whole. As an athlete, your experience of the zone is a direct communication that you have pushed yourself to the outer edge of your limits, the outer edge of your physical ability. You have reached an important milestone and are ready to go even further.

The practice of meditation is also a practice for experiencing the zone. Like the zone, it's an altered state of consciousness. The more you practice, the more you sharpen your focus and calm your mind, the greater the likelihood that you will enter a flow, a state of steady awareness and effortless concentration. The more you experience this state, the easier it is to return to it. A consistent practice prepares you for breakthrough experiences not just during training or athletic performance but in every aspect of your life.

Practice Your Way to Ultimate

To get the most from the chapters to come, approach this book with an open mind, insurmountable faith, focus, and commitment. Use the knowledge you gain as a tool and apply it so that you can honestly evaluate its impact.

By absorbing the ideas presented here and practicing the exercises provided as consistently as you can, you will begin to align your body, mind, and spirit, emotions, and energy into a synchronicity that will eventually unfold into a flow. Like a flower from a seed, your efforts will empower the athlete in you to reach the level of ultimate—the top of your potential. Are you ready to take your game to the highest level you can imagine? There's an infinitesimal difference between being good and being great, so small that it's easy to overlook. This book will help you jump that gap.

THE FOUNDATION
Practicing Mindfulness and Meditation

Mindfulness and meditation have been around for thousands of years, since humans first became aware that they had a consciousness. Before there were books or written guidance, humans connected with the world and themselves in ritualistic ways. Evidence suggests that early humans may have chanted and prayed, and some anthropologists speculate that hunter-gatherer societies got their first taste of meditation when staring at the flames of their fires. This was the source of their strength, how they evolved into the incredible and intelligent human beings we are today.

When thinking about the focus of this book, I kept asking myself how athletes connect to the deep part inside themselves that leads to focus and flow and optimal performance. What makes an ultimate athlete? On the most basic level, a rigorous, cutting-edge fitness routine combined with mental muscle-building and discipline will bring success to every part of your life. When people focus on their mental fitness, they are better able to meet and then surpass their physical goals. Mental muscle is the key to self-discipline, delayed gratification, perseverance, inner peace, and strength. These are the skills you need to become the most physically and mentally effective version of yourself. After all, your body won't do what your mind doesn't tell it. But how does an athlete find the strength within to go even further, to reach the ultimate? The answer is by practicing mindfulness, deep contemplation, and meditation.

A Brief History

The word *meditation* comes from the Latin word *meditatum*, which means "to ponder." Now why is that important? By understanding the origin of the word, this allows you to comprehend that it has no affiliation with religion; it was a practice and always a practice that became misunderstood over time. Now, with this understanding, you can begin to open your mindset to the information presented in this book and possibly dispel any preconceived notions you may have had.

Around five thousand years ago, in India, authors of the Hindu sacred texts known as the *Vedas* recorded the first written discussions of meditation practice, which they felt were direct revelations from God. The origins of Buddhism can be traced to the teachings of a prince named Siddhartha Gautama who decided to give up all his possessions and search for the meaning of life. His enlightenment as the Buddha is said to have occurred while sitting in contemplation under a bodhi tree. Over time these and other stories of enlightened beings spread throughout the world, inspiring more and more curious people to explore the value of mindfulness. The awareness of this innate ability has been passed from our ancestors through story and our DNA right up to this current moment.

In the US there have been numerous teachers who traveled from the East to teach meditation. Paramahansa Yogananda was the first and one of the most influential, arriving here from India in 1920. His teachings focused on the ancient practice of Kriya Yoga, which was based on techniques for moving energy effortlessly through the body in a way that would bring the practitioner closer to "God realization." His book *Autobiography of a Yogi* has sold millions of copies since it was first published in 1946.

Transcendental Meditation (TM) was introduced to the US in the 1950s by Maharishi Mahesh Yogi, who became a favorite of the Beatles and the Rolling Stones. TM traditionally consists of two 20-minute sitting meditation sessions a day, during which the practitioner repeats a mantra. It remains a popular practice worldwide. In the 1970s Harvard Medical School professor Herbert Benson researched and wrote about the "relaxation response," while Jon Kabat-Zinn founded the meditation-based Stress Reduction Clinic. In short, meditation had arrived.

Since then the practices of mindfulness and meditation have grown exponentially and are starting to become an accepted part of everyday life all over the world. As *Time* magazine noted on the very first page of its 2018 special edition, The New Mindfulness,

> *Mindfulness has become the goalpost of modern life, the answer to our high-paced, overstretched schedules. Do you know anyone who doesn't want to be "more mindful" in some aspect of their life? Just search for "meditation" in the App Store and you will find a mind-expanding number of apps intended to help you plug into the here and now.*[2]

The important thing I want you to know is that meditation is not a religion, or a religious substitute, or a philosophy. You don't need a guru. You just need to develop a simple practice every day to get results. It's a proven way to cultivate focus, concentration, emotional intelligence, awareness, tranquility, and more. Period. As therapy, meditation has also been found to improve everything from anxiety and depression to sleep disorders and pain management. Applied to athletic performance, there is growing evidence that mindfulness and meditation can improve results.

> Meditation is not a religion, or a religious substitute, or a philosophy. You don't need a guru. You just need to develop a simple practice every day to get results.

What Are Mindfulness and Meditation?

When I talk about mindfulness and meditation, I'm basically talking about them as tools for becoming more conscious of our bodies, our thoughts and emotions, our inner spirit, and the overall quality of energy we bring to manifesting and living our life—what the Chinese define as our life force, what others might call our inner vibration, and what I described in the introduction as our Inner-G. These different components affect the quality and effectiveness of our actions, our ability to envision a goal and creatively achieve it. Mindfulness and meditation, while closely related, are not the same, but they complement one another. One cannot exist without the other. Both are needed to reach our highest potential.

Mindfulness is a state of active awareness, of paying attention to the present moment. When you're mindful, you observe your thoughts and feelings without judging them as good or bad. But this is not a passive state. Instead of watching your life pass you by, you engage with it in a new way, awakening to each experience. Mindfulness can be practiced anywhere, at any time, while doing anything.

Meditation is a more intentional practice where the focus is inward and the goal is creating a space of quiet openness and stillness, focusing mostly on your breath—slowly in, slowly out. There are actually many types of meditation. Some, for example, are designed simply to promote relaxation; others can lead to a heightened sense of well-being. Most of them have four things in common:

- a quiet location with as few distractions as possible

- a comfortable posture (sitting, lying down, even walking)

- a focus of attention (a chosen word or set of words, an object, or just following the breath)

- an open attitude (letting distractions come and go naturally without judging them)

I also like what Osho said about meditation. Known as Bhagwan Shree Rajneesh, he was an Indian guru who was both controversial and revered. He described meditation as

A very simple phenomenon. When you are not doing anything at all, bodily, mentally. You simply are. That's what medita-tion is. You cannot do it. You cannot practice it. You can only understand it. So whenever you have time for it, just be and drop all doing. Thinking is doing. Contemplation is doing.

Concentration is doing. Focusing is doing. Simply seeing all that is happening around you. You are not the doer. You are the watcher. That's the whole secret of meditation.[3]

Again, meditation is not a religious ideology, a philosophical doctrine, or a lifestyle change. It's a practice, a technique that gives you access to a level of extreme focus, effortless concentration, acute awareness, and serene tranquility. These states exist in everyone, at all times, but they are a by-product of meditation; you experience these benefits only after you find that stillness within.

It's often been said that mindfulness is the awareness of "some thing" and meditation is the awareness of "no thing," but I learned meditation as a tool for focusing on "one thing." For me the ultimate goal of meditation is to release all unnecessary thoughts so the mind can focus on and contemplate one thing and hold it there. Contemplation takes you deeper into whatever it is you want to explore. Another, more active form of contemplation is visualization: mentally concentrating on an image from either the past—what you've done—or the future—what you want to achieve. As an athlete, it may be perfecting a technique or sustaining motivation. These are both powerful tools for the ultimate athlete.

The Benefits for Athletes

I was introduced to meditation in high school but didn't really get serious about it until my junior year in college. After getting drafted into the NFL, I visited a monastery in the Ozark Mountains in Arkansas with a group of monks, which deepened my meditation practice. To play football at that level, I needed to ratchet up my game, knowing that my effort would be as much mental as physical. I started rewatching some of the karate movies I loved as a kid—*Crouching Tiger, Hidden Dragon*; *The Last Airbender*; *Kung Fu Hustle*—and they began to make more sense to me. I had the same experience with animated series such as *The Legend of Korra* and the *Kung Fu Panda* movies. Each of them had golden nuggets of wisdom connected to being aware and present, to being a warrior. My body would experience a surge of energy from the crown of my head to my feet, which inspired me further to meditate. I wanted to keep cultivating this special sensation.

Then I discovered that a lot of world-class athletes and coaches use some form of meditation or high-level concentration as part of their psychological and physical training routine. It's a long list that includes Kobe Bryant, Calvin Johnson Jr., Alex Honnold, Tiger Woods, LeBron James, Michael Jordan, Michael Phelps, Usain Bolt, Serena Williams, Venus Williams, Derek Jeter, and one of the best volleyball duos to ever play the sport—Misty May-Treanor and Kerri Walsh—as well as many others in nearly every sport.

Hall of Fame and eleven time NBA Champion basketball coach Phil Jackson introduced meditation to the Los Angeles Lakers and Chicago Bulls. Pete Carroll coached the Seattle Seahawks to a 2014 Super Bowl victory and used meditation as a tool for helping players get into the zone. There are lots of other examples.

In addition to physical preparedness, it's critically important for athletes to be mentally prepared. No matter how well you've trained physically, if your head isn't right and your emotions are out of balance, all that training could be wasted. The primary benefits of meditation—focus and calm—put athletes into the right space for optimal results and performance:

- You are less distracted by anxiety, fear, and useless thoughts.

- You don't easily succumb to pressure.

- You are more likely to keep your cool.

- You react to setbacks not with frustration but with creativity.

- You instinctively adapt to changing conditions.

- You aren't as hard on yourself if you make mistakes.

In short, your mind is clear, your body is ready, and it's easier to find your flow. Focus and calm are a potent combination! But don't just take my word for it. As you will see in the chapters to come, there are a growing number of studies linking meditation and mindfulness with positive attitudes, reduced anxiety, and improved performance. A recent academic review of this research titled "The Effect of Mindfulness and Meditation in Sports Performance" concluded that

> *[O]ne of the most important aspects of sports performance is the athlete's ability to train the mind to put themselves in the best situation to compete. This can come in many different forms. Mindfulness and meditation are the main focus. Many different theories have been studied. It is important to train the mind just as you would train the body. Using mindfulness techniques have been shown to increase athletic ability and focus . . . [and] increase performance and the athletes' ability to cope with inner and external stimuli to increase the competitive edge.*[4]

It makes sense, doesn't it? The way our minds work is central to our experience of life and sports, so let's use these tools to help retrain our thoughts and emotions to support us in our quest for the ultimate.

> There are a growing number of studies linking meditation and mindfulness with positive attitudes, reduced anxiety, and improved performance.

Not Just for Athletes

I know that I've been describing this book as about mindfulness for athletes, but I want to point out that the tips and insights I'm sharing here are not just for athletes. We are all athletes, competing and struggling and achieving in the game of life. All of us have a mind, a body, and a spirit, along with energy and emotions that constantly interact with the world around us and create the experience we have of that world. Sometimes that experience is beautiful. Sometimes it's hard. But always those experiences are shaped by the patterns inside us, influenced by the health of our body, mind, and spirit, which means the techniques and exercises in this book are applicable to everyone. And as evolving human beings, we are all inevitably returning to the enduring quest of our ancestors—to know the self.

In thinking about our loved ones, our families, and the people closest to us, we should always value the time we spend with them. The quality of that time has a direct correlation to the strength of the bond that we share. These bonds allow us to have truthful and intimate relationships, which help us to understand each other's motivations, behaviors, and desires. A commitment to keep building these relationships further compels us to predict, analyze, and improve those motivations, behaviors, and desires. As this cycle repeats itself, and when done with the best intentions, these bonds keep getting stronger.

Now, think about the amount of time you spend with yourself becoming aware of what's going on inside you. If you can't accurately predict, analyze, and improve your own motivations, behaviors, and desires—even with the best intentions—you will have a more difficult time finding harmony with others. And the less time you spend with yourself, the more likely it is that this will be the case.

Unfortunately, most people *don't* spend enough time with themselves. Between work, family, social media, and entertainment, we live in a state of nearly constant distraction that affects how we feel and react to the world. We forget that we have an internal compass that can guide us wisely. Fortunately, meditation provides an opportunity to get back in touch with that, but you need to make the time to do it, just as you make time for other people. It's just as important to get to know yourself as it is to get to know others. In this way meditation is a very practical tool. It brings greater mindfulness to your inner self and allows access to higher levels of concentration, awareness, and calmness that grow from inside the body and extend outward, like a seedling breaking soil.

All Life Is a Meditation

From a certain perspective, meditation works no differently than life. From the moment you are born to the moment you die, your life is a meditation. As we grow up, we learn different tools for how to navigate this world and be successful. You create goals and milestones for yourself and seek to achieve them. Along the way you run into bumps in the road, distractions, and pitfalls that steer you away from the goals you set out to achieve. You must bring your attention back to *your* goals and milestones and then stay focused on them. An interesting study from Harvard published in 2010 reported that 2,250 people tracked by an iPhone app spent an average of 47 percent of their waking hours thinking about something other than what they were doing! And much of that thinking time was focused on unpleasant thoughts.[5] This is not a good training strategy to accomplish what you want in life!

The same thing happens in mindfulness and meditation practice. Whatever intentions you set, your mind and body will inevitably distract you with conflicting thoughts, physical aches, external noises, and so on. You must then gently bring your focus back to your intention, often more than once. An important difference between the intentional practice of meditation and life's meditation is that in life, you can get stuck in states of frustration as you struggle to figure things out. When frustrations bubble up in meditation, staying stuck is not an option. You are taught to calmly shift your concentration back to the initial goal. Once you get the hang of just being and breathing, it becomes a habit that may eventually become part of everyday life. You start living and enjoying it better as your patience and concentration grow.

Meditation may sound easy, but it's not—at least not at first. As you start, it may seem like one of the most boring things you could possibly do. But the more you practice, the easier it gets, and when you come out of deep meditation, you feel alive, and the world around you becomes more vivid. And it's free! The benefits may not come right away, which can be frustrating in this culture of immediate gratification, but patience will reward you. Start by creating a simple goal, such as focusing on your breath for a count of thirty. Apply determination, consistency, and a little self-discipline. Before you know it, you will have built a habit and a consistent meditation practice and ultimately become more mindful. Make time for meditation in the same way you make time for other people. No excuses!

Practice, Practice, Practice

Again, meditation does not belong to a sect, class, religion, or region of the world. It is not a philosophy or a religious substitution. It is an effortless practice that helps cultivate and balance your energy and emotions, your body, mind and spirit. When you pay more attention to your life in this way, you become more mindful of your strengths as well as your weaknesses and more able to build on those strengths and improve those weaknesses. The key to both meditation and mindfulness is the breath, which is also the key to life itself. Your breath is the bridge that links it all. It's the difference between being alive and being deceased.

Of course this is obvious, so why is it so important for the ultimate athlete to remember? Well, if you're no longer breathing and a part of this world, you will never become the athlete you are capable of being. But you *are* here, and you *are* breathing. With every waking day full of breath and life, you have an opportunity to improve, to enrich, to succeed, to evolve your athletic performance to a higher level. And that is a gift.

Mindfulness and Meditation Basics

There are different positions you can use to meditate. Find the one that is most comfortable for you where you can also stay alert. Most pictures you see are of people sitting cross-legged on a floor, but not everyone can do this easily. If you try the floor, it helps to sit on a cushion. You can also sit in a chair or even lie down, but be careful: You want to be comfortable for meditation, but not so comfortable that you fall asleep and you miss your meditation!

Note: Always keep your spine erect and straight whether lying down or sitting upright.

The Breath Cycle

Your breath is the bridge that links everything: your body, mind, spirit, emotions, and energy. It's the key to living—without it, you perish. The breath cycle provides a way to align these five components while recalibrating and refining your focus. Like a warm-up exercise for the physical body, the breath cycle is preparation for transitioning into a mindful and meditative space. As you go through this book, revisit this breath cycle exercise to remind yourself of the importance of being present.

Various thoughts and distractions will take your attention away from your breath. That's okay. No matter what they are, gently allow them to come and go, without attachment, like passing clouds, and return your attention to your breath.

As you stay focused on your breathing, your thoughts dissolve, and you will begin to relax. I recommend starting this exercise with a goal of just one to two minutes, eventually working your way up; there is no limit. Each time you practice, look to improve your posture, control of your breath, your duration, and focus. Set a timer for yourself and once your timer goes off, slowly bring your awareness back to the room around you, and when you're ready, gently get up and continue your day.

However long you meditate, the goal is to be fully committed and to practice regularly, at least six days a week without a break between days. It can help to do it at the same time every day.

Now, it's time to start practicing. Find a comfortable position where you can settle into a quiet location and follow these steps:

- Make sure your spine is erect.
- Close your eyes.
- Now focus on your breath. The natural inhale and the exhale.
- Breathe in through your nostrils to the back of your throat as deeply as possible, inhaling as much air as you can.
- Hold your breath for five to eight seconds.
- With control, exhale all the air from your lungs.
- Repeat these steps two more times. Then allow for your body to relax.
- Now simply sit as still as you can for the duration of your intended time, while breathing naturally—in and out, in and out.

POWER

When we think of power, we usually imagine having power over something or "bigger is better." And that's still how most people think about it. But true power emanates from within. It may take power to push a tire up a hill, but it also takes power to be patient when patience is called for or to accept oneself in the face of apparent failure. True power is quiet, not loud. It is a state of disciplined awareness and realized potential. This is the kind of power that the ultimate athlete strives for.

THE BODY

It's not about being the strongest and the biggest. It's really about what are you going to do with your strength. And what are you going to do with the power that you have.
—PATRIK BABOUMIAN
(GERMANY'S STRONGEST MAN, 2011)

For an ultimate athlete, what is the purpose of the body? To perform optimally. As an athlete, I know that we tend to concentrate on the functioning of the body above all else, sometimes to the detriment of the mind and the spirit. This chapter will introduce techniques that will help bring you back to your core self and help align the body with the mind and spirit, which will ultimately lead to the zone of high performance. This alignment will also help you find the balance between power and peace, between taking action and being still.

Most athletes think of the body as the doer because all our experiences happen through the body. This is logical and true. But when we understand that our bodies are living tools helping us to accomplish a goal or reach a destination, we develop a new appreciation instead of measuring its value by the number of pounds it can bench press. This doesn't mean that physical abilities aren't important; it's all about how you get there.

I've been fortunate to work for many years with two physical trainers, James Cooper and Tom Bender. Early in my professional career, they would say to me, "Prince, the most important thing to consider when it comes to your body is to see it as a vehicle. Are you a high-performance car or a low-performance car? Once you decide which one, you'll know what type of fuel to put into it, either premium gasoline (optimal nutritional food) or regular gasoline (unhealthy food)." That saying stuck with me, and I finally realized that an athlete needs to see the body as a precision machine and not as a horse to overwork. That's when I really started paying more attention to my body and what I put into it, which led me to value and cultivate the role of mindfulness in my life. If I didn't pay attention to what my body was saying, it wouldn't get what it needed to take me where I wanted it to go.

I learned that the body is intimately connected to the mind and the spirit. What do I mean by that? If you consider each of the three on a scale of importance in descending order with spirit at the top, followed by the mind and then the body, it would be confusing. But when you understand that your spirit inspires you to act upon a desire or goal, which activates your mind, which then puts the body into action, the relationship between the three is seen as cooperative, not hierarchical. They all work together to help you fulfill your life's purpose.

When your spirit, which I define as the life source within every living organism, has a purpose or a goal it wants to achieve, it starts to work with the mind—both its conscious and subconscious aspects—to figure out how to accomplish it. The mind then starts calculating strategies and projecting thoughts as it looks for the best way forward. Slowly but surely, the body will take those thoughts and do its part to help make that intended goal a reality. In a sense the actions of the body are a by-product of what the spirit and mind direct it to do.

Another way of looking at this is to imagine that our thoughts are like seeds that need fertile soil to sink their roots in and then precipitation to grow. That precipitation, that driving force, comes in the form of our emotions (e.g., desire, enthusiasm, commitment, determination, persistence), which begin to germinate those thoughts in the body. Seeds also need the light and heat of the sun to help break out of the soil and become the fruit, flower, or tree they are intended to be. For athletes—for anyone—that sun energy happens when we take specific actions, such as training and optimal nutrition, to manifest our goals. When a seed—a thought, an intention, a goal—is planted in the right environment, it opens and flourishes, even in harsh conditions.

As an athlete, it's important to understand how this body-mind-spirit process works. Each has a role to play. When they are in alignment and working together, your ability to manifest, to optimally perform, to reach the zone, accelerates. Take a few moments to ponder this. Imagine in detail how such an understanding will start to change your life.

> When a seed—a thought, an intention, a goal—is planted in the right environment, it opens and flourishes, even in harsh conditions.

Learning to Communicate with the Body

The tools of mindfulness and meditation help athletes learn how to listen to the body's needs and the body's voice. Yes, the body has a voice. It talks to the brain all the time, and we need to be aware of what it's saying. When we were young, we didn't listen to the body as much as we should have because there were so many other distractions and no one taught us how important it was to care for the body. Sitting quietly for a few minutes in meditation is an excellent way to practice and develop those listening skills. Over time you will begin to learn how to communicate with your body; you will come to know what it wants—and what it doesn't want. This takes time because your body is one of the most complex organisms on the planet, and the clues to what it needs aren't always so obvious. Physical training and exertion alone are not enough to take you where you want to go. Figuring out what else is needed takes listening, mental discipline, and practice. But when you put all those pieces together, you can accomplish almost anything.

In addition to practicing mindfulness and meditation, another great way to establish a healthy awareness of our body's voice is through yoga. Yoga, which means "union with the self," originated in India thousands of years ago as a philosophy of living that included physical, mental, and spiritual practices. Most athletes know yoga only as a way to help stretch the body, and that it does, but there are far more benefits to yoga than just a good stretch. The most important has to do with connecting the body with the mind, which for the majority of athletes has never been experienced. Fortunately, as yoga has become more popular, opportunities to experience that connection and communication have become more common. Breathing and mindfulness, which help strengthen the connection between the mind and the body, are central to yoga and central to becoming an ultimate athlete.

The key when practicing yoga is to rhythmically elongate your breath when stretching into and out of bodily postures. This improves seven things:

- breath control
- mental control
- balance
- protection against injuries
- endurance
- mind–body connection
- blood flow

As you get in touch with your breathing, you will begin to sense the body's energies. This will improve the way you take care of it because you will become more aware of what it needs and then take the proper steps to provide that. The regular practice of yoga will continue to build that mind-body-spirit connection and support your goal of becoming the ultimate athlete.

Caring for the Body

Once you've developed reliable, mature, and consistent communication with your body, the actions you take will be that much more successful. Athletes tend to think of the body as a well-oiled machine that requires little maintenance, like the Energizer bunny—it just keeps going. But for your body to sustain its ability to perform at a very high level, you need to take care of it, and no detail is too small. Ideally this starts at an early stage in your life, but the majority of athletes weren't taught how to properly care for the body unless their parents were athletes or other mentors were around to assist. For most, optimal caretaking only begins when such awareness is brought to their attention. Fortunately, it's never too late!

Let's start with nutrition. Many of us have heard the adage "You are what you eat." This is absolutely true. What we put into our bodies will directly correlate with how well we perform in our sport. It also influences how quickly the body recovers from injuries and helps to prevent them in the first place. When it comes to deciding what to put in your body, think of it as that high-performance vehicle I mentioned earlier. Proper nutrition is critical, though the best approach will, of course, vary for different people.

After my rookie year in the NFL, I started seeing how my body responded to certain foods. I would notice a difference, for example, in how I felt when drinking fruits and vegetables instead of eating them, and I started making more smoothies and juicing.

When I first started working with my trainers, Tom and James put me on a strict diet of protein, salad (no dressing!), and fruit and vegetables. I could feel how my body missed my usual eating habits, which was to eat whatever I wanted. Not that it was all bad, but I craved those honey buns! The following training season, I noticed a difference because I now had something to compare myself to, how I felt the year before versus how I felt in my second year. My aha moment came when I realized that I was in even better shape and I felt great! My body had responded beautifully, still sculpted and strong after months of eating a more nutritious (and very different) diet: fewer carbohydrates (e.g., bread, pasta), more fish, chicken, vegetables, and fruits, smaller portions, and almost no fried or processed food. Everything in moderation. It was all about balance.

I also avoided too much red meat, which made me sluggish. That was hard because I've always enjoyed a big, juicy burger! But I found leaner, high-protein alternatives such as bison and more plant-based options. It turns out that more and more elite athletes are switching to low-meat and even vegetarian diets because the research is showing that they can keep you leaner and more energized, reduce inflammation, lower blood pressure and the likelihood of heart disease, enhance your performance, and help you recover faster. Olympic cyclist Dotsie Bausch and NBA All-Star Andre Iguodala are just a few of many athletes who swear by these approaches.[6][7][8] I also learned that when I ate was just as important as what I ate. Most calories should be consumed earlier in the day rather than later. No more late-night carb loads.

Proper hydration is another important component of a successful training routine. Getting enough water before, during, and after exercise will help you recover more quickly, avoid injuries, and achieve peak performance. Good hydration is everything; it regulates your body temperature and digestive system, helps your muscles grow and absorb more oxygen, and lubricates your joints. It helps move nutrients through your body, which gives you energy and keeps you healthy. If you're not hydrated, your body can't perform at its highest level. It's been recommended that, depending on the sport and training routine, athletes need to drink one hundred ounces or more of water a day, or one ounce for every two pounds of weight. And don't wait until you're thirsty, because it might be too late! The more regularly you hydrate, the greater the benefit.

> It's critical to pamper your body. You only have one, and the better you take care of it, the more reliably it will take care of you and perform at a high level.

I can't emphasize this enough—it's critical to pamper your body. You only have one, and the better you take care of it, the more reliably it will take care of you and perform at a high level. Getting plenty of rest, proper nutrition, regular hydration, stretching, going on hikes or walks along a beach, stimulating mind and spirit by reading thoughtful and inspirational books—these are perfect ways for the ultimate athlete to develop a loving relationship with their body and all of life while strengthening their mind–body connection.

Ultimately, the objective of most exercise and training programs is to strengthen the body's core, which includes thirty-five muscle groups in your hips, lower back, quadriceps, gluteus, groin, and abdominals. Yoga is an excellent practice not just for general stretching and mind–body connecting but for getting you to focus on your core, which is necessary to hold those difficult poses. It also brings you back to your breath.

Core exercises helped me to lower my time in the forty-yard dash from 4.56 to 4.27 seconds in just six weeks. But I did them consistently and diligently, either before or after practice. Your experience won't be exactly the same as mine, whatever you're trying to achieve—it may even be better! But I know that the following core exercise will activate those thirty-five muscle groups to increase your speed, agility, and overall strength.

How Mindfulness Serves the Body

Let's return to the definition of mindfulness. It's a state of active, open attention on the present moment. When you're mindful, you observe your thoughts and feelings from a distance, without judging them as good or bad. Instead of letting your life pass you by, mindfulness creates an immediacy, an active engagement with everything that's happening in the moment. You awaken to life's experiences instead of sleepwalking through them.

When you practice mindfulness, you become acutely aware of your thoughts and the present moment without judgment or attachment. When applied to the body, mindfulness opens up channels of information and feedback for how to use your body (your vehicle) properly. This is the first step in what I call "internal engineering," which is about working on yourself and building confidence from the ground up, from the inside out. When you follow such a path, there is nothing you cannot accomplish with the body, clearing the way on your ultimate athletic journey.

When you learn how to observe your thoughts from a distance and not judge them or label them good or bad, your mind begins to relax. When your mind makes less noise, your body functions slow down enough that your body's voice can more easily be heard. As you learn what it needs, you respond by satisfying those needs, and in the process, the body shows its appreciation by functioning better. With a mindful attitude, the systems of your body will start working together more successfully and harmoniously.

> Mindfulness creates an immediacy, an active engagement with everything that's happening in the moment. You awaken to life's experiences instead of sleepwalking through them.

Recall the metaphor of seeing the body as either a high- or a low-performance vehicle and how that influences what you do to it and for it. In thinking about the practice of mindfulness, let's extend that metaphor to what a person needs to know to take that vehicle from one destination to another.

When you get into a car, it doesn't just leave and take you where you want to go. First you turn the key in the ignition. Then you let the car warm up. You turn on the navigation system and enter an address. Then you take it out of park and follow the directions given. Along the journey there are stop signs and stoplights, bumps and potholes, maybe even accidents or speeding ambulances that need to be avoided. In order to do so, you have to be focused on what you're doing. That's how you safely arrive at your destination. When first learning to drive a car, such skills don't come naturally or easily. But as you practice, you become more comfortable and relaxed, mindful of the obstacles and distractions. You and your vehicle begin to operate at a high level of efficiency and performance.

Now apply that same analogy to learning the art of mindfulness. The idea can seem kind of intimidating at first. Going within ourselves to slow down and pay attention, getting in touch with something we don't fully understand, takes some getting used to. But the more mindful you become of your vehicle (the body), the more aware you become of your speed bumps, stop signs, potholes, distractions, and so on that make it more difficult to get from where you are to where you want to go. As you learn how to focus, concentrate, and pay attention, you also start getting in touch with your intuition, which, like the internal navigation system of a car, makes it even easier to reach your destination. Once you learn how to go within yourself and become more mindful, an experience of relaxed awareness emerges. As you practice this, it has a big impact on your day-to-day life. You become better equipped to anticipate and respond to any obstacle that arises.

Mindfulness, then, is about becoming aware of being aware, and it happens when your eyes are open. Mindfulness is also the doorway into meditation, which will bring you even closer to your goal of ultimate performance. In a way mindfulness preps the engine of your mind by slowing down your thoughts, getting it ready for the meditative journey that will gradually take you from Point A (normal awareness) to Point B (deep awareness).

How Meditation Serves the Body

Meditation works alongside mindfulness and happens when your eyes are closed. When you meditate, you either focus on one thought or observe all of them while staying detached and refraining from judgment. You simply see them for what they are.

Meditation still has a bit of a stigma for some, a kind of woo-woo quality. And it looks a bit weird: Why are people just sitting there? But when you sit in meditation, you aren't just hanging out with your eyes closed; you are often wrestling with your mind and emotions, two of the hardest things to gain control of. But once you do, you can achieve some incredible things in the realm of competition and elsewhere in your life. Said another way, when your mind is settled and focused, it can be your greatest ally; when your mind is unsettled and unfocused, it can be your greatest enemy.

Since meditation was brought to the West some decades ago, there have been quite a few studies on its benefits. The practice of meditation has been shown to improve focus and attention, discipline, emotional management, and levels of stress and anxiety. (I'll say more about this research in the next chapter.) Some studies have found that prolonged meditation practice can even change certain parts of the brain! This phenomenon has a name, *neuroplasticity,* which basically means the ability of the brain to form new neural pathways that can aid functions such as memory and learning.

I've talked a little bit about the important role of inner peace in one's life, which you will also read more about later in the book. It's a quality I discovered while going through my own transitions and challenges. And so I was truly excited when I found out that research studies determined that one of the primary benefits of meditation was the achievement of equanimity—mental and emotional steadiness, staying focused and on track, staying cool no matter what's going on in your life or in the arena of competition. This inner balance ties all the other benefits together while improving physical well-being and aiding in the accomplishment of your goals.

So now we know that meditation helps us to relax, focus, and better organize our thoughts. There is also what I call advanced meditation, which will take you beyond that initial level of benefits and closer to a deeper level of physical, mental, and spiritual fitness.

Advanced meditation means diving deeper into yourself for a glimpse of what you're truly capable of. It puts you in touch with the core of your being and unleashes instinctual and intuitive capacities you never thought possible. How does one get there? Practice. Repetition is the father of learning. Pause for a minute and experience what it's like to just sit and contemplate, to focus gently on one thing. It's not so easy! But it's no different from how a period of intense training is required to break through to new levels. At first it's hard and frustrating. You keep pushing against something, and it keeps pushing back. After a while, though, as you keep practicing, you start to see gains, and then the gains come more easily, and your confidence grows. *I can do this*, you start to realize. *I'm good and getting better*. You begin to see your performance—and your potential—from a different perspective.

This is similar to advanced meditation, although it's not a competition and there is no failure. There is only the path forward. So after creating a habit of meditating five minutes every other day, for example, you might transition to ten minutes every day, then fifteen minutes, then twenty, and so on. Over time you reach that place of quiet awareness more quickly, more deeply, and more effortlessly while sustaining it for longer periods. During this process you are also cultivating and conserving your energy like a samurai warrior. Ultimately, without the distractions of your thoughts and emotions, your intuition becomes more available, and a sense of peace emerges. You start getting in touch with your Inner-G, and your access to the zone opens up. It becomes a part of you and you a part of it. The zone you reach in advanced meditation is no different from the zone you aspire to as an athlete. The experience is essentially the same. The training of the mind and the training of the body go hand in hand, and an ultimate athlete needs both.

> When your mind is settled and focused, it can be your greatest ally; when your mind is unsettled and unfocused, it can be your greatest enemy.

When you begin your meditation practice, you will notice how it slows down your thoughts and calms your mind. Over time the consistent practice of meditation will calm down the entire body. Once you calm the entire body, you can focus your energy in whatever direction is most helpful to you. Said another way, the more you meditate, the calmer your nerves will become. It will then be easier to tap into your Inner-G and intuit how best to achieve an optimal level of performance, no matter your sport. For example:

- In basketball, improving your free throw percentage or perfecting your jump shot.

- In American football, running better routes or making those difficult throws, catches, or tackles.

- In tennis, adding speed and accuracy to your serve.

- Working on your spin, rotation, slam, and location in table tennis.

- Perfecting your baseball torque and swing and bat–ball contact.

- Adding distance and accuracy to your golf shot.

- Dropping your time on the track or on the road.

- In soccer, working on your dribble and shots.

There are many such examples; the practice of meditation can help them all. I'm emphasizing the word "practice" here. In the same way that practice helps you refine your skills and game, the practice of meditation will help you go deeper and gain more benefit from it. The first step is the key: Set a specific time each day and stick to it as best you can. When you do, your simple practice will turn into an experienced and then an advanced practice, which will allow you to do more than just play your sport—it will help you excel. You will reach the ultimate level not just in your sport but in your entire life.

Optimal Care, Optimal Performance

Again, for an ultimate athlete, what is the purpose of the body? To consistently perform at an optimal level. What role does the aspiring ultimate athlete play in that? Staying healthy and being conscious of what you put into your body. Keeping the immune system strong, conditioning the nervous system to be calm and collected no matter the situation, and giving your body proper nutrition, hydration, and rest.

The body is remarkably resilient. You can ding it up, run it into the dirt, fill it with unhealthy things, and it still keeps ticking. It will heal itself with just a bit of rest and water and without asking for your permission. That's a miracle. And it's what makes the body different from a car; you can constantly improve and refine it. A car can only take so many dings and so much use before you have to replace it.

Remember, your body carries out the directives of your mind and spirit. Your spirit ignites the process by inspiring you to become all that you can be. Your mind starts working on how to convert that inspiration into manifested reality. Your body is the last to get the message, but it will get it and play its part.

When to Meditate

There are two ideal times to practice meditation to improve performance: right before or after a workout, practice, or game. Both have different purposes.

When you meditate before an activity, your goals would be to calm your nerves and focus your mind, set your intentions, and visualize what you want to accomplish. Maybe it's perfecting a movement, reaching a certain speed, doing a rep, or maybe it's the number of reps of a certain activity. It can be anything you choose to concentrate on with the goal of then achieving it. If you have film of yourself training or competing, watch yourself closely in a nonjudgmental way and then follow that video session with meditation. Focus your energy on the gaps between what you see and what you intend, and then visualize the movements or techniques you want.

Meditation after an activity is the perfect time to power back down and recall what you experienced or accomplished. The body's muscle memory retains its last activity, and when using meditation to assess or fine-tune performance, you want to be able to connect with that. This concept is similar to what happens in education when students attend a lecture. Once the lecture is over, students can be expected to retain only 5 percent of what they heard. This compares to retaining 10 percent of what is read, 20 percent from an audiovisual presentation, 30 percent from an actual demonstration, 75 percent from practicing what is learned, and 90 percent when immediately teaching someone else. In short, the more involved the student becomes in the content, the sooner they develop mastery of it.

The same thing goes for the body when you meditate immediately after a workout, practice, game, or performance. The experience is fresh, and you're better able to learn from how you did and build on that knowledge when preparing for the next activity or goal. Also, when the body is exhausted or near exhaustion, it can more easily sit still because most of your energy has been burned off. The mind can then use the residual energy left in the body to reflect on what was accomplished, what needs to be accomplished, and what skills need refining. This will help solidify your vision of what you want to achieve. Focus in particular on recalling anything you felt good about—especially if you experienced the zone—so the memory of that is reinforced and absorbed into the body, the mind, and the spirit.

Used in these ways, meditation becomes the refinement process to help you align your mind, body, and spirit and balance power and peace for the purpose of reaching the zone.

Sitting Still

This basic exercise may seem silly, but it's fundamental to developing a successful meditation and mindfulness practice.

Take a series of three slow, deep breaths followed by slow exhales— the basic breath cycle as described in the previous chapter. Observe how your body starts to relax. Continue the cycle until you feel your body has settled.

Now stay still—completely still. Start with a goal of ten seconds and pay attention to your body. Did you move? Keep practicing and building the duration until you've disciplined yourself to sitting completely still for one minute. As you keep up this practice, keep lengthening that period of stillness.

Cultivating Energy

The following meditation helps to propel the energies of the body, mind, spirit, and emotional intelligence toward a certain level of maturity. The goal is to create a place where the zone becomes the natural state of an ultimate athlete's life.

Find a comfortable place, such as reclining in a chair, lying on the floor, or sitting on a meditation pillow. Gently stretch the entire body one area at a time: the arms, neck, shoulders, legs, ankles, hips, hands, and anywhere else that you feel could use some loosening up. Take your time, and really focus on each area.

Then go through the breath cycle at least three times and allow the body to relax deeper with each exhale. You can also do the tension relaxation technique of tensing and holding different muscle groups and body parts for a count of five and then releasing them, starting with your feet and work towards your head, including your facial muscles. Don't forget any!

Close your eyes, sit quietly, and witness whatever thoughts arise. Try your best to disconnect any emotions from your thoughts. Even if you experience something that makes you happy or sad or mad, continue to sit and observe as if you are looking at a blossoming flower. The steadiness of holding the flower in your mind helps to keep your mind steady. Your goal is to become aware of what emotions arise and then watch them dissolve as you inhale and exhale. Remember, the goal is not to clear your mind, but to observe your thoughts and emotions without judgment. I like to use the analogy of observing your thoughts and emotions like an air traffic controller is aware of the arrival and departure of planes, weather, wind patterns, and flow of traffic. Try to do this for two to five minutes and build from there.

Building Your Core

This three-part exercise, which you should do every day during the season either before or after practice, will help increase your speed and improve your agility by helping to align your hips, lower torso, quads, hamstrings, knees, calves, and feet.

Note: Once the core is activated, the rest of your body will function the way you intend and train it to—optimally and at full capacity.

Begin by lying on the floor on your side with your hips stacked and your back, gluteus, and heels of your feet against the wall.

First: With your upper leg, do a series of straight leg lifts up along the wall, making sure your foot stays in the same neutral position. You should feel tension in the back and the buttocks.

(three sets of twenty-five reps)

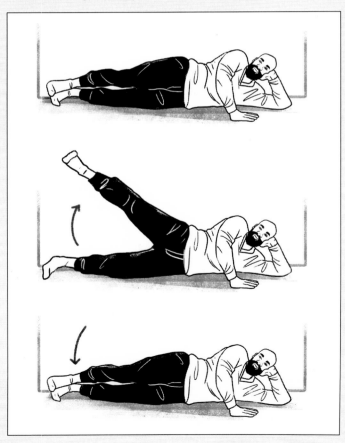

Second: With the heels of your feet still against the wall, lift from the hips and raise the top knee from the bottom knee without taking your foot off the wall—the legs should look like two sides of a triangle, with the wall being the base of the triangle. Again, you should feel tension in the back and the buttocks.

(three sets of twenty-five reps)

Third: Raise your knee to your chest as if you're running but do it slowly and with control, as if you are balancing something on the outside of the thigh near the knee. I sometimes place a roll of duct tape or a rolled-up towel on top of the knee as a way to maintain that slow control. Make sure that the knee and leg are in a perfect 90-degree angle when raised to the chest and that your back and buttocks are engaged. This is a powerful hip control exercise that will increase your speed and vertical strength. To make this even more challenging, go back to zero if the tape or towel falls off!

(three sets of twenty-five reps)

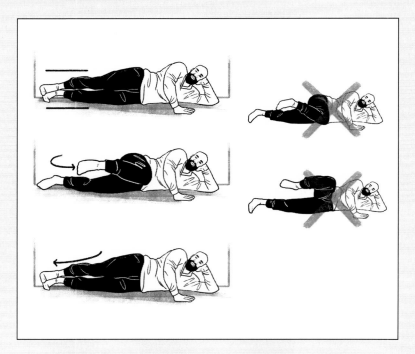

Note: Do all three exercises on one leg, then flip over and do the other leg. Work your way up to doing three sets of reps on each leg.

THE MIND

Imagination is more important than knowledge.
For knowledge is limited to all we now know and
understand, while imagination embraces the entire world,
and all there ever will be to know and understand.
—ALBERT EINSTEIN

The spirit is the master of the whole being. The heart is the master of the mind. The mind is the master of the body. All of them work together to help you fulfill your goals and purpose in life, whatever they may be. And because you are reading this book, that purpose includes pushing yourself to a degree of athletic performance you have yet to experience. What you focus on with your mind and fuel with your energy and emotions will crystallize, so you want that focus to be clear and those emotions to be healthy.

The Mind–Brain Connection

In the previous chapter, I talked about the body and how it benefits from a practice of mindfulness and meditation. I also discussed the tight connection between the body, the mind, and the spirit. In this chapter I will focus on what happens to the mind when you make a commitment to these practices and how those changes will lead to improved training and performance.

When you talk about the mind, in many ways you are talking about the brain. You literally can't have one without the other, but they are not the same thing. One way to think of it is that the mind is the software and the brain is the hardware. The mind generally includes all of our cognitive functions, such as thinking, motivation, perception, judgment, and consciousness. It drives how we see, interpret, and react to the world around us. In your mind you experience imagination, recognition, and appreciation. It processes feelings and emotions that lead to attitudes and actions. But none of this is possible without the hardwiring of the brain.

> The spirit is the master of the whole being. The heart is the master of the mind. The mind is the master of the body.

The brain works like a big computer, but it's far more complex. It's roughly the size of two clenched fists and weighs a little over three pounds. From the outside it looks a bit like a large walnut, with lots of folds and crevices. There are about 100 billion nerve cells (neurons) in the brain and one trillion other cells that have their own specific functions. There are four main parts of the brain:

- The front—and largest—part of the brain is called the *cerebrum*. It controls reading, thinking, learning, and speech as well as vision, hearing, and other senses. It has a left and a right hemisphere to control the right and left sides of the body connected by an area called the corpus callosum. Think of it as the engine control system.

- The *cerebellum*, in the back of the brain, is primarily a movement control center that handles balance, coordination, and fine motor control (e.g., writing or using a fork). It also functions to maintain posture and equilibrium.

- The *amygdala* is the main processing center of our emotions, where we experience "fight or flight." It's located in the deep center of the cerebrum above the brain stem.

- The *brain stem*, at the bottom of the brain, connects the cerebrum with the spinal cord. It controls automatic body functions such as breathing, eye movements, blood pressure, heartbeat, and swallowing.

The brain and mind work closely together, and meditation affects them both. The brain is also the bridge between the mind and the body. Using the tools of the brain, the mind creates thoughts and emotions, which the brain then translates into action, either outwardly or inwardly focused, and sometimes without our awareness. Excessive anxiety, for example, will cause the brain to send signals of stress to the heart, which can lead to health problems. Positive emotions will have an opposite effect. Motivation will put our bodies into gear, getting us up and out for that early morning run. Depression will keep us in bed.

Developing Your Athlete's Brain

So what does all this have to do with athletes and, more importantly, meditation? A few years ago, an article came out titled "The Brain: Why Athletes Are Geniuses." It started with a great quote I'll never forget: "The qualities that set a great athlete apart from the rest of us lie not just in the muscles and the lungs but also between the ears."[9] It went on to explain that great athletes do what they do because, in addition to being both highly skilled and physically prepared, they have a unique ability to make split-second decisions and respond immediately—instinctively—to quickly changing conditions. How do they do this? By processing information better and faster, whether it's in the moment or during training. And how do they do that? They're able to minimize distractions, which optimizes that ability to process data.

> "The qualities that set a great athlete apart from the rest of us lie not just in the muscles and the lungs but also between the ears."

When, for example, the brain waves of karate champions at rest were compared to those of ordinary people, researchers found that "the athletes emitted stronger alpha waves, which indicate a restful state. This finding suggests that an athlete's brain is like a race car idling in neutral, ready to spring into action."[10] In another study done by the same research team, they monitored the brains of pistol shooters under several conditions and concluded that "when the pistol shooters hit their target, their brains tended to be quieter than when they missed." Fewer distractions, greater focus—better results![10]

And how do those brains get so quiet? Physical training and skill-building help, of course. As soon as someone starts learning a new skill or sport, the brain responds immediately as new pathways of information exchange open up. As you get better, the brain doesn't work as hard. But another kind of training is necessary to reach that level of ultimate: mind training. The normal mind is constantly racing with thoughts and emotions, jumping from one to another. The term for that is "monkey mind." It keeps us from focusing on the present moment, and when you're training or competing, a monkey mind will sabotage you, and all it takes is a split second. So the goal is to get it under control.

Think of your mind as a muscle that gets better and more efficient with mental exercise. The right training reorganizes the brain in a way that reduces unhealthy and unnecessary thoughts, emotions, and patterns of behavior and replaces them with healthier ones. It can also reduce the actual number of those thoughts and emotions. When the mind is too busy, it takes energy from the body. A study published in the *Journal of Applied Physiology* found that cognitive fatigue—thinking too much or too intensely—limited athletic performance.[11] People who were given heavy cognitive tasks before a time-to-exhaustion cycling workout could only cycle for an average of 640 seconds, while individuals who didn't perform those tasks cycled for an average of 754 seconds. That's a big difference.

Now, let's talk a little more about your brain. There are five kinds of brain wave:

- **Delta** (<4 Hz) are the slowest—this is the frequency when you are sleeping.

- **Theta** (4–8 Hz) occur when your mind is still or when you're in deep meditation, giving you access to creativity and intuition.

- **Alpha** (8–13 Hz) represent the resting state of the brain, when you're quietly alert or doing yoga.

- **Beta** (13–32 Hz) are our day-to-day brain waves, when the brain is active and engaged.

- **Gamma** (32–100 Hz), the most recently discovered, are the highest-frequency brain waves and still a mystery. They've been observed in long-term meditators, in states of love and altruism, and during mental peak performance—when one is operating in the zone. Ironically, research has also discovered that the quieter the mind, the easier it is to access this high-frequency state.

> The mind is a gym, and meditation is the workout that will accelerate your potential for achieving ultimate performance.

As you can see, the brain states that give us the best chance to unleash the highest-performing parts of ourselves rely on a quiet mind.

Meditation Changes the Brain

As mentioned in the previous chapter, the ability of the brain to change shape and grow new connections in response to new and repeated experiences is called neuroplasticity. The high-performing athlete's brain looks different from a normal person's brain because, over time, it has been upgraded and fine-tuned to operate at a high level as a result of intense physical training and disciplined practice. But those aren't the only activities that contribute to positive changes in the brain. New research shows that meditation also affects the physical structures of the brain in a way that helps athletes access their higher potential. While the meditating athlete experiences changes in their thoughts and emotions on a conscious, mental level, the structures of their brain are changing at an unconscious level. As the mind and the brain work in tandem, the ability to process information, control emotions, and minimize distractions improves, which leads to better and better performance.

This doesn't happen overnight, but it does happen, and research at prestigious universities proves it:

- In one study that compared the brain images of fifty adults who meditate to those of fifty adults who don't, researchers found that the meditators had more folds in the outer layer of the brain (something called *gyrification*), which increases the brain's ability to process information.[12]

- Another study found that meditation thickened certain areas in the cerebral cortex, leading to higher pain thresholds.[13]

- Researchers also found that meditation decreased the size of the amygdala (our emotional center—the caveman brain), lowered its electrical activity, and reduced levels of fear, worry, and anxiety.[14]

There are others. It's heavy stuff, but it's important. These studies show that meditation and mindfulness practices affect both your mind and your body. They change the physical structures of your brain and help turn your gray matter into a high-performing athlete's brain by improving your ability to react and make split-second decisions, recognize patterns, visualize goals more vividly, minimize unnecessary thoughts, control emotions, and focus. Said differently, the mind is a gym, and meditation is the workout that will accelerate your potential for achieving ultimate performance.

TIP » Breathing and Stress

Any time you start to feel stressed out, breathing can come to the rescue. Deep, full inhales and exhales calm the amygdala—the emotional center of your brain—and help you think and remember more clearly. Pay close attention to how you feel both before and after you complete a minimum of four such inhales and exhales.

The Power of Focus and Positive Thinking

So now we've established that the mind and brain are intimately connected, that certain changes in the brain can improve athletic performance, and that those changes are accelerated by meditation and mindfulness. And though the brain is a complicated, impressive piece of machinery, it doesn't do us much good unless it's activated in some way. And so, in the same way that gasoline powers the engine of a car to take us where we want to go, thoughts and emotions power our brains to take us where we want to go—or sometimes where we don't want to go unless we start paying attention to them.

How does the mind get so caught up in unnecessary thoughts and emotions, to the point where it becomes a debilitating force? It's because the average mind is easily distracted by external influences outside of one's control. It's built to respond to stimuli. This was a good thing for evolution because if a caveman suddenly saw a tiger out of the corner of his eye, he would need to react quickly. But these days it isn't tigers getting our attention but everything else, from our cell phones to billboards to honking cars to thinking about what to cook for dinner—the list is huge and getting longer as information technology takes over more and more of our lives. One thought or distraction quickly leads to another and then another, and before you know it, you become lost in them.

Even when you sleep at night, there is still energy in the body—it's not completely exhausted. That residual energy transfers to the mind, making it more active, which then turns those thoughts and energies into dreams. Your mind never sleeps or stops working; it keeps busy, it keeps going. That mental energy also replenishes while sleeping and is waiting for you in the morning. Who wakes up with an empty mind and a clean slate? Almost as soon as you open your eyes, those thoughts and emotions go to work.

That constant chattering is fuel for our livelihood and existence. It's good to have a strong mind. It's designed to have thoughts, ideas, and emotions. But it can also be your biggest obstacle when those thoughts and ideas are out of control and taking over your life. Having a mute button for the mind is imperative.

Some of the problem may be boredom. We all get bored. And what happens when we're bored? The mind drifts, we start thinking of other things, we try to escape the present moment. But when you're focused, on task, and committed to a goal, those distractions have a lot less appeal.

One of the first steps to changing course is mindfulness—simply being aware that we are being distracted. As you develop this ability, it's helpful to ask yourself from time to time, *Are these thoughts and emotions the ones I want? Will they take me where I want to go?* One way or another, we're going to have thoughts, we're going to have emotions, so why not give ourselves the power to choose and make them positive and focused on a goal, whether it's athletic performance, self-improvement, or both? Remember that gamma waves, the highest-frequency brain waves, only happen during positive states of love and altruism and during peak mental performance.

You've probably heard of the placebo effect. It's a medical term that describes the phenomenon of people recovering from a health condition after being administered a drug that they aren't aware is fake. The power of the belief that they were taking something they were told would help them was enough to trigger their innate self-healing abilities. Well, there's also something called the *nocebo effect*, which describes the opposite: When you hear something negative enough times, even if it isn't true, you come to believe it, and then it becomes a reality. This almost happened to me.

When I was nineteen, I was a walk-on football player at Georgia Tech. A walk-on is someone who is neither recruited nor awarded a financial scholarship but can still practice with the team. As a walk-on, you don't get treated fairly, and one coach in particular didn't like me, his name was Bill O'Brien. He repeatedly told me that I was too mechanical, that I wasn't what they were looking for, that I would never be a starting running back and definitely never play in the NFL. Oh, and I would never get a scholarship. To be honest, the odds were definitely against me; I was seventh on the depth chart at running back, which meant there were six scholar-ship players in front of me and I might as well have been a tackling dummy. Still, there was nothing fair about how I was treated, and my frustration over circumstances I couldn't control began to grow into rage.

Shortly after our spring game, we took an evaluation and exit exam before the summer break. The coach reiterated everything he'd said at the beginning of the season. He said I sucked as a foot-ball player and to get the [expletive] out of his office. I left feeling infuriated, debased, crushed, and hurt. I stormed to my bus stop, and it seemed that time had stopped. I just sat there trying to figure out why this was happening to me, what I had done to deserve this fate. Then I realized that it wasn't anything *I* did. My father had taught me this is how the real world works. It can be cruel and mean. And you can't control everything. But there was one thing I could control—me. And I had this inspirational realization: "I will not allow anyone to take my dream away from me. This is *my* dream."

From that moment on, I dedicated myself to making my dream a reality. I stopped feeling sorry for myself, tightened the straps of my backpack, and took off running across the entire campus as tears streamed down my face. When I got back to my dorm, I threw my pack on the floor, put on my workout clothes, and ran to the volley-ball sandpit where the 1996 Olympians practiced and played. I ran drills and sprints until I nearly passed out and kept it up through the summer, working super hard—sometimes to the point of uncon-sciousness—all while keeping a positive attitude. In the end, my perseverance paid off, and I eventually became Georgia Tech's starting running back. In 2004 I set an NCAA record for the most rushing yards in a bowl game with 311 yards (along with four touch-downs), a mark that still stands today. I ended up the fifth leading rusher in Georgia Tech history and was drafted by the Baltimore Ravens in 2006. I was deeply grateful but knew I had earned it, not just because of my physical training but from using my mind to keep me focused on my goal to prove the naysayers wrong and drawing from my spirit and that of my teammates for inspiration.

The power of the mind to accomplish such things is awesome and available to everyone, but you sometimes need help to get there and then to stay on track. A good way to start is to think of your thoughts as mental seeds and your emotions as the nourishment that will make them grow. What seeds do you to plant? What seeds are you *going to* plant? What do you want to accomplish in this world? What training and performance goals do you want to achieve? Increasing your ability to focus on these commitments is one of the main benefits of meditation. It creates the space for new inspiration to sink roots and grow. As your mind becomes clearer, you will waste less time on distracting thoughts and emotions and start moving more creatively and efficiently toward accomplishing your goals and dreams.

> Think of your thoughts as mental seeds and your emotions as the nourishment that will make them grow. What seeds do you *want* to plant? What seeds are you *going* to plant?

Mastering the Fundamentals

The ultimate athlete depends on the fitness of both body and mind. The physical training, while challenging, is straightforward enough: effort, repetition, doing what it takes to prepare the body to perform at a high level. That could mean a range of routines in the gym such as stretching and weightlifting, extra miles on the track or on uphill runs, the constant practice of specific skills and moves—whatever it takes to get that edge.

It's no different with the mind. Everyone can think, but not everyone has refined their mind to think and make decisions at an optimal level. It too is a muscle that needs to be exercised if it's to help you reach an ultimate level of performance. For example, mental repetitions of focusing or holding a specific thought or image in place is the equivalent of doing push-ups, pull-ups, sit-ups, or squats. The more you do it, the better you get, and the more quickly you'll improve your mind and brain and your powers of concentration.

In his book *Outliers*, Malcolm Gladwell writes about people who achieve mastery by doing the same thing repeatedly for literally thousands of hours. I would call this concentrated-focus meditation. It strengthens the brain, which essentially strengthens the mind. When one then applies the knowledge acquired, the integration of body and mind is complete, holistic.

Doing other things like reading, solving puzzles, and playing memory games will also stretch your mental abilities. I'm a big fan of reading, especially when you read to learn or for self-development instead of for entertainment. Such reading requires focus, concentration, retention, and comprehension. Then it becomes the equivalent of doing physical exercise because it takes effort to absorb what you read and then apply what was learned. Reading this book, for example, is strengthening your mental fortitude and bandwidth while improving your ability to be aware and mindful.

> As any true athlete knows, to get to the next level, you have to master the fundamentals. But to get to the highest level, you have to master the intangible, the unknown.

My favorite way to strengthen the mind, though, is practices that emphasize *being*. The practice of being—focusing on a single thought or thinking of nothing at all—is more difficult than it sounds. Try it now. Pick a single thought, or let your mind go completely blank, and then stay there. Not so easy.

Such practices don't come naturally to the way our brains have evolved over eons or how our minds have been conditioned from birth to absorb and process all the stimulation that comes at us from all directions. And so, to really experience the benefits, you have to approach it like any physical exercise, such as running or lifting—practice makes better, and more focused and efficient practice makes ultimate. As any true athlete knows, to get to the next level, you have to master the fundamentals. But to get to the highest level, you have to master the intangible, the unknown. So think of meditation as a fundamental part of your training routine. As you practice, your mind will begin to change in the following ways:

1. reduced stress
2. well-ordered and rational thinking
3. improved intellectual and intuitive skills
4. a heightened sense of awareness that helps you see the bigger arena of play
5. a calmer brain and calmer mind
6. fewer distractions
7. increased focus and concentration
8. sharper memory
9. an integrated awareness of your path forward

Of course, it's not just your training and performance that benefit; your entire life will begin to change for the better as well. Now imagine trying to meet your training and performance goals without the benefits of a fit and healthy mind. You still might get there, but the road will be steeper, and it will take longer to arrive.

Overcoming Limits

It's a good time to talk about limits. Everything I've been saying so far assumes that you are essentially unlimited in reaching your goals if you attend to both the mind and body with commitment and perseverance. I do believe that, and my belief comes from experience. But to get to ultimate, limits will be reached, and they will need to be overcome. To go beyond them can feel extremely difficult, if not impossible. When you reach a limit, you feel lost, convinced that you can't advance any further than where you are. Nevertheless, when those limits are met, part of your purpose is to find a way past them.

Fortunately, as you build your practice, you are developing four important tools: letting go, observation, deep contemplation, and intuition/imagination. Each of them plays an important role in helping you overcome limits and reach that next level.

1. **Letting Go.** The first thing that usually happens when you meet a limit is that emotions are triggered: anger, frustration, despair. Emotions cloud your judgment and decision-making. They want your attention; they distract you from what is happening in the moment. They make it difficult to see a situation clearly, both what it is and how to get through it. If unattended, they will keep you from exceeding those limitations. The first step is to let go of them, to sit calmly and allow them to dissipate. What's left will simply be a thought. Thought + emotion = manifestation. To manifest a way beyond your limits, first remove negative emotions. The mind will be more at peace, which will magnify your perspective and make it easier to see the nature of the challenge in front of you.

2. **Observation.** The act of observing is natural to who we are. We are constantly observing or being observed. This is how we learn. In dealing with a limitation, you need to be centered enough to see it because you won't always know what to look for. Once you let go of your emotions, you are able to observe whatever is keeping you from moving forward with some detachment. Think of it as information-gathering; maybe there's a mental block or a pattern of fear and anxiety, or an area of tightness or physical resistance, or an old injury that hasn't quite healed. A *Beginner's Guide to Meditation* has this advice: "In meditation, we are trying to get the mind to work effortlessly. At first, however, it takes effort. Therefore, the beginning phase of meditation is concentration. You must, with effort, focus your mind upon something until you discipline the mind, and then 'let go' so that the mind will flow into the solution."[15]

3. **Deep contemplation.** Once you've identified the nature of the limitation you're facing, the next step is what I call deep contemplation. You are no longer focusing a laser on the obstacle but letting go of that concentration and gently

sitting in meditation with what you've discovered. This will create a space beyond logic and analysis, where solutions often emerge. That space is often described as the source of our intuition and imagination.

4. **Intuition/Imagination**. Meditation and deep contemplation bring the two hemispheres of your brain, logic/analysis and creativity/intuition, together in balance. This is done by activating what is called the *corpus callosum*, a thick band of nerves that connects the two.[16] When using these tools, you are no longer trying to think through a limitation or problem but allowing a solution to emerge. Perhaps something comes to you right away, or maybe it takes a few sessions. When you finally get an answer, use your imagination to lock it into place and gently visualize next steps. This process of intuition/imagination/visualization creates a powerful template for new habits to develop. It also begins to train you for experiencing the zone, which depends in part on both concentration and letting go.

One of the major roles of meditation is refinement: using your experiences, imagination, muscle memory, knowledge, and breath to work through challenges and keep improving. By focusing on something for an extended period of time using the process described above and visualizing the details again and again, you start to correct faulty fundamentals and ingrain optimal performance into your mind. This is a common tool for world-class athletes to condition their minds and brains for ultimate success. World Cup and Olympic medalists such as Canadian bobsledder Lyndon Rush, American freestyle skier Emily Cook, and one of the greatest Olympians of all time, American swimmer Michael Phelps, are just a few who have used different forms of contemplation and visualization to achieve their dreams. And it's not just athletes, but leading-edge coaches all over the world in nearly every sport teach their athletes these tools.

The Achievement of Athletic Genius

Visualize yourself being in an airplane thirty thousand feet above the ground. When you're that high, those buildings on the ground don't seem so huge—they look small and insignificant. The same thing happens to your problems and your worries when you meditate; it puts distance and perspective between you and those everyday concerns so you can focus more clearly on what you really want to accomplish. Those repetitive cycles of self-defeating negative emotions and debilitating thoughts are cleared from the mind.

In the process of going deeper inside yourself, you're not only preparing the mind to work more closely with the body to take your athletic aspirations to the highest level, you're also raising your frequency and vibration and intuitive abilities. Meditation builds confidence in your mind and your whole being. As you get more comfortable with who you are, you start to accept your flaws and insecurities, the choices and mistakes you've made, as just that. They do not define you. They are not a measure of your self-worth.

> Few know that being aware is what helps make an athlete a genius, someone who sees the game from the inside out as well as the outside in.

Always remember, if you're doing the right thing, the right results will naturally flower in your life, not because you're being rewarded but because this is the natural law of the universe. Athletes who meditate understand this on both a conscious and a more subtle level. They accept that there will be struggles, sacrifices, and turmoil—that's how you overcome obstacles and grow—but there will also be triumphs. The only requirement is to consistently follow a routine that nourishes your body, mind, and spirit.

Being calm, focused, aware, and prepared during competition is the goal of every athlete. It gives them the edge. They understand precisely how to balance effort and energy: not too much, not too little. From the perspective of others watching them perform, they look like a genius. However, few know that being aware is what helps make an athlete a genius, someone who sees the game from the inside out as well as the outside in. Whether they are on a stage or a platform, on a beach or a field, in a coliseum, gymnasium, natatorium, or Olympic arena, the ultimate athlete has found a silence within and a depth so riveting that their minds are crystal clear and their bodies are ready. They are completely in the moment and connected. For them, there are no limitations.

The mastery of power depends on bringing the mind and the body together in movement. The mastery of peace, which I will describe in more detail in the next half of the book, relies on elevating your spirit and then bringing all the elements together to experience the zone. When you have found your perfect balance of power and peace, you will have attained the level of ultimate.

Exercise Your Mind Muscle

Find a quiet space and bring a blank sheet of paper or journal with you. Take a few moments to breathe and do one full breath cycle to allow your thoughts to settle. Next, follow these steps:

1. Write or draw your primary goal or vision (in life or in your sport) at the top of the page.

2. Now write down as many ideas as you can for how to reach or even expand that goal. What are you not doing? How have you been holding yourself back?

3. Over time, you will do some, release some, and keep updating your list. Add more goals! What is the vision you have for yourself? Employ both logic and your imagination. You'll be amazed at what you come up with, and no idea is too small.

4. Now put this in a place where you will see it every day to strengthen your attraction to your goals.

Remember, successful people are not without problems. They're just better than most at solving them. Don't waste time and energy worrying about unnecessary distractions or what you aren't achieving. Use your mind effectively to break those patterns and achieve your dreams!

Count Your Breaths

This exercise will improve your ability to focus and concentrate. Most people think the two are the same thing, but they aren't. Focus is the ability to put all of your attention into the task at hand, moment to moment. Concentration is the ability to finish something from start to finish. This exercise strengthens both.

Note: This exercise may take some time to get used to, but once you find the rhythm, it becomes automatic.

- Set a timer for five minutes, using one that shows seconds (e.g., a stopwatch).
- For thirty seconds, as you naturally inhale and exhale, count only your exhales.
- For another thirty seconds, count only your inhales.
- Do each of these five times, one right after the other.
- If you get distracted and lose count, calmly start over.

If the timer runs out before you finish, that's okay, because the goal is not to beat the timer. The goal is to pay keen attention to the rhythm of your breath while counting.

Once you're comfortable counting with your eyes open, try doing the same exercise with your eyes closed. (But don't forget to set the timer!)

Mind–Body Integration: Mastery of Movement

During my professional years, I would sometimes make a minor mistake and get reprimanded by my head coach, Brian Billick. "P. J., you are smarter than that," he would say. "You went to Georgia Tech, for crying out loud. Use that engineering mind to master this game." It wasn't enough that I was fit or had learned the playbook or watched a training film. I had to test both my mental and physical skills in real life—in this case on the field. But I had difficulties bringing the mental side of the game together with the physical. In meetings I learned all about the Xs and Os, where everyone should line up, and my particular responsibilities, but when I got onto the field, I would sometimes forget.

Whenever you exert energy at high intensity, your core muscles become activated and contract. In order for me to think more clearly while competing on the field, I needed to come up with an exercise that connected my core and my brain so that my game prep recall became second nature. To master the merging of the mental and the physical, I combined two exercises to simulate my movements on the field so I could simultaneously have the experience of being on the field physically and mentally. It involved tiring out my abdominal muscles while forcing my brain to download and act on critical information. And it worked! I was able to rewire my brain and enjoy the benefits of neuroplasticity. I gained a much better understanding of the game of football, and those Xs and Os in the playbook became much less intimidating. Here's how it works:

- Make flash cards of a subject that you want to study and learn.

- Do thirty sit-ups without reading or looking at the cards. This fatigues the abdominal muscles and simulates the core exertion you use when you run, swing, jump, swim, lift, and so on.

- Start reviewing your flash cards on the thirty-first repetition. Recite them out loud. Feel yourself memorizing the information. Stay focused on what you're learning and not so much on the pain—easier said than done!

- Keep breathing and controlling your breath—don't let it control you.

- The ultimate goal is to do one hundred sit-ups while memorizing, reciting out loud, and absorbing the information on the cards.

- Keep building the stamina of your body and mind until you reach one hundred sit-ups effortlessly. At this point you will have mastered this technique.

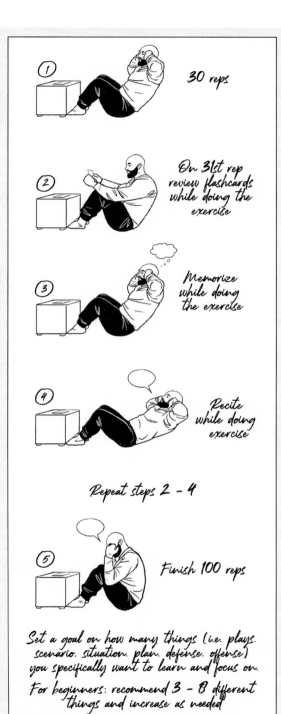

Visualization and Refinement

Meditation and visualization can be performed before and after an activity for different purposes. If your goal is to review and refine a technique or how you performed during a workout, game, or competition, the best time to meditate is directly after—win or lose, succeed or fail. The experience is fresh, and so your ability to focus on the results is enhanced.

Begin this exercise with the basic breath cycle of three slow, deep breaths in, followed by slow, controlled breaths out, feeling the body and mind relax deeper and deeper with each exhale. Close your eyes and allow yourself to feel all your senses without judgment. Imagine, in detail, what you've just finished, whether in competition or in training. Pay close attention to every move, every moment you can recall. This is an important exercise because your entire self—the body, brain, mind, emotions, and spirit—acts as a kind of hard drive that stores knowledge and experiences.

If what you did during training or competition was already perfect, if you were in the zone, focus on what made it so at all levels: the mind, the body, the spirit, the emotions. Be completely aware of your centeredness, calm, and supreme confidence. This will make it easier to retain that experience and return to it. If you fell short of your goal, keep visualizing the ideal result until you feel you have internalized it. This review-and-refinement process is tedious, but it's the key to mentally conceiving and then physically achieving. You can also apply this technique to your daily training regimen or any positive habit you want to add to your regular routine.

This can be a challenging exercise because you likely won't feel the subtle change. The process can be like observing the bud of a flower—patience is required. But that flower will bloom, and when it does, the beauty of it is impressive. Your performance will also bloom with consistent practice of this contemplative visualization. It puts you back in touch with the inspirational (in-spirit) spark that comes from inside you. It will also improve your ability to be mindful, expand the way you perceive things, and enhance muscle memory.

I suggest setting a timer for twenty minutes for this process, as the body may become stiff and distracting thoughts are likely to start up again. For some, at least at first, this may be too long; for others, twenty minutes won't be enough. Find your own rhythm and balance!

PEACE

To understand your true power, you have to believe in yourself and be at peace with yourself. It's a bigger challenge than running on a treadmill or lifting weights because there is no clear path to get there—everyone is different. The achievement of spiritual growth and the experience of living in the zone are not as well understood as what we know about the body or the mind. They are considered unknown frontiers. But the unknown is where you will discover your true potential; it's where you will find true peace. Fear of the unknown only exists when the unknown is avoided. That fear is dispelled when you embrace it.

THE SPIRIT

Quiet the mind, and the soul will speak.
—MA JAYA SATI BHAGAVATI

So far, we've talked about the ultimate athlete's body, brain, and mind. Each one has defining characteristics that separate the high-performing athlete from everyone else. They are, in most respects, tools. Wonderful, powerful tools that can take us to incredible heights. The spirit, however, is a different kind of force. Think of it as the energy that powers everything.

First, what do I mean when I use the word "spirit"? It's not an easy question to answer because it means different things to different people in different contexts. The word itself comes from the Latin word *spiritus*, which means "breath."

Here are two dictionary definitions of "spirit":

Merriam-Webster: "An animating or vital principle held to give life to physical organisms . . . the activating or essential principle influencing a person . . . a supernatural being or essence."

Oxford: "The non-physical part of a person which is the seat of emotions and character; the soul is the non-physical part of a person regarded as their true self and as capable of surviving physical death or separation."

They seem to be saying that spirit represents a force both inside us and outside us, something that gives life and is bigger than life. I've sometimes heard people wonder whether we are spiritual beings having a human experience or human beings having a spiritual experience. I believe it's the former. Everyone's body grows older and runs its life course. Our brains deteriorate once the body ceases. Our spirit, however, the essential part of us that gives us life, remains. It is eternal; it never dies. It just is. I also believe that every living being on planet Earth—not just humans, but all creatures—has a spirit.

Like the practice of meditation, spirit, as I understand it, has nothing to do with religion. There are different religions, but I believe there is only one spirit, one force, that animates all life. The goal is to allow it to become stronger, to have more of a presence. And I think that we all, consciously or unconsciously, seek this experience.

Have you ever thought about your heart? For me, the heart is the house of the spirit. The heart is the first body part that develops, along with the spinal cord. It starts working and becomes active before any other body part. It's the first thing doctors check when determining the health of a fetus.

> There are different religions, but I believe there is only one spirit, one force, that animates all life. The goal is to allow it to become stronger, to have more of a presence.

There is some very interesting research suggesting that the heart acts like a second brain, that in fact, the heart and the brain are in constant communication, affecting our emotions and how we think and perceive. An erratic heart rhythm, for example, correlates with difficulties reasoning, remembering, and making decisions. When the heart rate is strong and steady, you are more likely to experience positive feelings, emotional stability, and higher cognitive function.[17] [18]

And what powers the heart? Spirit. It's the electricity that vitalizes your existence. Our spirit is within our heart, and so whenever you become inspired to achieve a goal or purpose, that inspiration is coming from inside you, which makes sense. "Inspiration" derives from two words: "in" and "spirit." This power is available to everyone and anyone, but not everyone gets inspired, even fewer become inspired to be athletes, and fewer still are inspired to become ultimate athletes. It takes a lot of sacrifice and dedication, which is where the power of spirit comes into play.

I realized the importance of my spirit during my self-rehabilitation time. Not being able to finish my career as a professional athlete on my own terms made me dispirited. I became paralyzed and fearful of the unknown. I knew I needed to gain a stronger connection with myself, my internal self that I always felt was active and alive and connected to an infinite source but somehow lost. I just had to find it again. It was meditation that taught me to look within myself, focus, contemplate, and pray. I learned that I had a speck of light that had dimmed but never went out. If you practice focusing on that light inside of yourself, you will find that nurturing that light is like feeding a fire with wood and oxygen. I came to see how everyone in the world is connected, and paralysis eventually became movement. Fear became excitement.

The Ultimate Athlete's Spirit

The first section of this book focused on how mindfulness and meditation can help you listen to your body and become more aware of what it needs—and what it doesn't need. Your body is like a powerful but fine-tuned engine; you have to take care of it for optimal performance. You also learned how meditation trains the mind to focus and perform at a high level by lowering stress levels, reducing distractions, and creating a calmer disposition and a stronger focus. Now, you will learn about the importance of spirit and how meditation clears the mind so that the power of your indwelling spirit can emerge. Quieting of our thoughts makes it easier for the inspirations of our spirit to be felt.

To repeat the powerful words of George Leonard, "The athlete that dwells in each of us is more than an abstract ideal. It is a living presence that can change the way we feel and live. . . . [It is] the ideal unity of physical and spiritual."[1] As you become more in tune and connected to your spiritual self, you become more attuned to who you are and what you're supposed to do in this life, both as an athlete and as a human being. This is the missing piece: purpose, or what some might call a passion or a mission. Without something to get up for every day, the human spirit will atrophy and wither, along with all your goals. Spirit and purpose give you resilience for life's challenges. When you have those forces behind you, it's like adding an extra gear to the bike or a sharper edge to the ski—you can more easily overcome challenges or limitations and reach that next level. You're operating as a whole human being, no parts unused, and anything is possible.

> **As you become more in tune and connected to your spiritual self, you become more attuned to who you are and what you're supposed to do in this life, both as an athlete and as a human being.**

When an athlete is inspired toward a clear objective, whether or not they know how difficult it will be to get there, that's the work of spirit. It's that initial spark, the thing that makes you unique. The spirit then talks to the mind: "Let's do this!" The mind then says to the body, "Let's do this!" There may be resistance along the way, but the spirit and mind will keep working with the body to get it done.

An ultimate athlete's spirit is a champion's spirit: It looks to defy and surpass limitations. When an athlete focuses the entirety of their energy, emotions, body, mind, and spirit on an outcome, they enter a special realm. It means they are competing as much for the chance to be all they can be as for the achievement itself.

The Role of Meditation in Cultivating Spirit

When you practice mindfulness, it's with eyes open, exploring the external world with your senses engaged, using your mind to become aware and internalize what's going on outside of you. When you close your eyes, that's meditation. It forces you to go inside, where the orientation is different. Your attention is no longer focused on and attached to what you see and hear. It starts to look at itself, aware of all the thoughts, insecurities, faults, fears, and bodily sensations. As you sink below the surface level of these thoughts and sensations, you start to become aware of another level. Something alive, a spark of light that is unique to you. But since it's likely been neglected, the light is dim. It needs attention, like a small flame. You need to nurture it to help it grow. When that starts to happen, your presence, your energy, and your positivity grow, and you start to understand who you really are. You become a lot more conscious and self-aware. These changes are subtle at first, but like fitness gains, they get stronger over time with consistent practice.

When you begin to focus on your inner self, you will add a different dimension to your game. You'll be concerned less with conquering others and more about conquering yourself. That means conquering those limitations that are keeping you from being your best in competition and in everyday life.

To be clear, meditation is a different kind of workout. It doesn't have a specific goal; it's more a process of helping us to both concentrate and let go. Meditation doesn't train the spirit; it puts us closer in touch with the essence that is unique to each person. It allows our deeper, higher impulses to come forward. The ultimate athlete is not just fine-tuning their mind and body for competition but becoming an athlete for all of life. The spiritual benefits you experience when going deeper into a meditation practice—the spiritual fitness you cultivate—make you a better person. You are then able to apply those higher qualities to everything you do.

The Benefits of Spiritual Fitness

The road to becoming an ultimate athlete has three parts: physical fitness, mental fitness, and spiritual fitness. As athletes, we're taught to mend the body and mold the mind to serve a specific outcome. After defining your goal—the athletic performance you aspire to—you train your body, making it as strong and quick and flexible as possible. You feed and nurture it, work your muscles, build your lungs for respiratory endurance, and refine your skills.

That's physical fitness. Then you train your mind to concentrate and focus, to ignore distractions, to keep you on track. That's mental fitness. For most athletes that's where it ends. But there's a third pillar: spiritual fitness. Unfortunately, this pillar is often neglected. We know little about what it is and why it's important.

Again, the image of a samurai warrior brings a lot of what I've been describing together: the skill, the mental concentration, the discipline, the inner balance, the focus on the present moment. These are indispensable qualities, and all must be engaged. The famous Japanese sword master Yamada Jirokichi once said, "Sword and mind must be united. Technique by itself is insufficient, and spirit alone is not enough."[19] The samurai first had to conquer themselves before they could go into battle. They also had a code of ethics that put honor, loyalty, and service ahead of their own needs. They weren't just trained warriors; they were dedicated to something bigger.

The eighteenth-century samurai Yoshida Shoin, who was also a political activist, said, "Once the will is resolved, one's spirit is strengthened. Even a peasant's will is hard to deny, but a samurai of resolute will can sway ten thousand men."[20] The samurai didn't fight for themselves but for others, and only in a way that maintained their dignity in triumph or in loss. This can only come from a spiritual orientation, from being connected to the bigger picture. It's hard to imagine a retired samurai who didn't maintain those high standards. In some ways they never retired—their character endured no matter what they did next.

There is something unique about the athletic spirit: It has the ability to keep regenerating, to never give up—either on itself or on life—even in the most doubtful situations.

And so there is something unique about the athletic spirit: It has the ability to keep regenerating, to never give up—either on itself or on life—even in the most doubtful situations. Why is this so? It's not just because of the ability of the body to heal and go on or the mental discipline to ignore all obstacles. I know it's something more, attitudes and qualities that can be traced to spiritual fitness and that the ultimate athlete takes with them once the training and competition end. Those qualities might be different for everyone, but they will include at least some of the following:

- **Desire** follows inspiration. When your spirit inspires you toward a goal, desire is the emotion that embodies it and keeps you moving forward. It's more of an unconscious force than a conscious one.

- **Will** gives you the power to overcome obstacles and control those sabotaging emotions or actions. It's similar to desire but is more about the ability to make your own decisions. "I am going to do this. I will fulfill my purpose. I will persevere."

- **Self-motivation/self-validation**: I say "self" because the ultimate athlete doesn't rely on others to feel good about who they are and where they're headed. That doesn't mean they don't benefit from the love and support of others. But in the end, they will look to their own inner strength for purpose and meaning.

- **Courage**: Going forward in the face of pain, grief, fear, or failure is not a trained skill but a capacity that comes from being spiritually centered.

- **Patience/perseverance**: Spiritually centered athletes realize it takes time to scale great heights. They are steadfast and will do what they need to prepare. If there are setbacks, they accept them and keep going.

- **Intuition/anticipation**: When your spirit is active, a channel to other sources of information opens up. You start connecting more dots, and the quality of your preparation and performance improves.

- **Perspective**: Spiritual fitness gives ultimate athletes the ability to see the bigger picture from thirty thousand feet above the ground. An experience of failure is not the end of a story but an opportunity to learn, to grow, to recalibrate.

- **Inner tranquility**: When your mind is focused and your spirit is calm but aware, you experience a sense of peace. If you suffer a setback, or the world around you is in distress—or both!—you're able to keep your center and maintain equanimity.

- **Belief** is not the same as optimism. It gives you the ability to visualize success, to exceed your limits. There's a famous quote from Henry Ford: "Whether you think you can, or you think you can't—you're right." Nothing is impossible unless you believe it is.

When your unique spirit is activated, you are guaranteed to grow as a human being in the same way a seed grows into a flower:

- Appreciation for living is enhanced.

- Spiritual growth continues to progress naturally.

- Inspiration heightens and begins to positively affect others around you.

- The thought of everything working out for you becomes a reality.

Ultimate in Sports and in Life

For the first few years after we're born, we still have a strong connection to our spirit. But as we grow older, worldly things weaken that connection. We start using less of our spirit and more of our body and mind to go through life. This is not a bad thing; we need to understand and experience how the mind and body function, and that can only happen in real life. As an athlete, this emphasis on body and mind to reach your goals is natural. It's what we've been trained to do. And for many that's enough. But for most, that emphasis has come at the expense of the spirit, and that's the missing piece that will elevate you to becoming ultimate.

Why does this matter? Athletes learn a lot about life and themselves through sports, including leadership skills, teamwork, selflessness, dedication, commitment, and self-awareness. They also learn a lot about what it takes to compete at a high level, the endless drive to never give up. The ultimate athlete is under tremendous pressure to bring all their physical and mental forces together to accomplish a hard-to-reach goal. It's far more arduous than anything the average person endures. How do they stay with it? Is a trained body enough? Is a sharp mind enough? To get to the top of your game, there needs to be one more piece—the spirit. And for the aspiring athlete, that means a quality of character and commitment that is bigger than themselves. This is important, because you don't have to do any kind of spiritual work to perform well in sports. There are plenty of athletes who have mastered their skill without the knowledge of spiritual fitness. But why aspire to just that? Why waste the gifts you've been given by not living up to your potential? Ultimate means excellence not just in how you perform but in who you are.

Preparation for the Zone

The sweet spot—how do you find it? How much time are you willing to dedicate to your practice to get there? Two, five, ten, twenty, thirty minutes? Can you maintain that practice every day? These words are not meant to be a challenge but an encouragement. No one tries to build a mansion in one day. A house is built brick by brick. The difference between building a house and building your meditation and mindfulness practice is that home-building has a start and a finish, but your contemplative practice has no limitations. It

> The difference between building a house and building your meditation and mindfulness practice is that home-building has a start and a finish, but your contemplative practice has no limitations.

continues as long as you choose; the only limitations are the ones that you set. You just need to start somewhere and slowly build it with discipline and consistency.

All the words and exercises in this chapter are designed to connect you with your spirit, with your inner source of inspiration, and to make that connection continuous. Meditation focuses your attention on the deeper impulse that is unique to you and the source of your true power. The more time you dedicate to meditation and inner practices, the faster and deeper you will develop this connection. It becomes part of your everyday life. This will support you both as a competitor and as a human being.

You can now start to see how the body, mind, and spirit work together to take you where you want to go. It's not a hierarchical relationship but a cooperative one where everything is interconnected, where the feedback loops are continuous. Getting to the top requires that you optimize both your athletic and personal potential because each one plays a necessary role. The road to ultimate is steep, and there will be times when you just don't think you can go on, when the body or the mind is fatigued. This is when the gifts of the spirit are most critical. When athletes push their body and their mind beyond the limitations they didn't think they could get past, that's the work of the in-spirit. So cultivating its power, its fitness, should become part of every training routine.

And more than that, to reach the zone, your body, mind, heart, spirit, emotions, and energy must all be balanced. When they click together, a door opens to something magical. You are no longer you in the usual sense but something else, a flow, an experience. Let's learn more about this in the next chapter.

Daily Contemplation

I did this while I was in the NFL. I would wake up every morning no matter my mood—tired, happy, sad, mad, out of whack—and do this simple exercise. During my meditation I would ask myself: "What is my focus for the day? What am I looking to accomplish?" Although I never knew exactly how this was benefiting me, I always came out of the meditation with a new perspective and fresh energy. I actually stopped for a week to see what effect that might have, which was difficult because I had created a daily habit, and observed subtle declines in my mood. I restarted the practice, and that's when my understanding of the Xs and Os and the intricacies of the game of football began to accelerate.

For just a few minutes each day, when you wake up or right before bed, find a comfortable place to sit where you can relax. Then inhale through the nostrils as deeply as possible, hold the breath for a three-second count (silently count one one thousand, two one thousand, and so on), and slowly exhale through the mouth with control, exhausting all the air from your lungs using your diaphragm. Repeat this three times.

Try to do this at the same time and, if possible, in the same place every day, and slowly increase the time you do it based on your level of comfort. No candles, incense, or altars are required; simply close your eyes, breathe in and out, and allow your body functions and mind to calm down. As they do, take a moment to feel a sense of gratitude for your life and the opportunity to improve your craft. You can also use this time to contemplate and hold a vision for how you want your day to look and feel. What is your spirit saying to you? This is the time to listen. Once you establish a habit of this routine, you will catch a rhythm that is in synchronicity with the universe. Everything has a rhythm, everything has a frequency, a rhythm that its energy vibrates in; an ebb and flow, and the universe is no different.

Positive Affirmations

We all recycle mind chatter and self-talk for most of any given day. Much of that talk is negative, aimless, or simply a reaction to a given situation. That's why it's important to spend time repeating things that are positive, that give us energy, that start to reprogram us for success.

The following affirmations are designed to break those negative cycles and set you on a new course. Take time during the day to repeat them. You can also record yourself saying these words and then play it back in the morning before you start the day or before bed. It's powerful to hear them in your own voice.

After relaxing your body and mind with the breath cycle, repeat the following affirmations and pause two or three seconds between each one:

- I am grateful for _____.
- I am supremely confident in my abilities as a _____ (your sport/position).
- I am assertive and thoughtful in my decision-making.
- I am strong.
- I am graceful.
- I am always focused under pressure.
- I am in total awareness.
- I am free of debilitating thoughts and fears.
- I am anchored in the zone and present in the moment.
- I am synchronized with my higher self and my highest aspirations.
- Learning to relax will improve the skills I have refined through meditation.

After you're done, take a deep breath, sit in silent contemplation for a few minutes as you allow these words to sink in.

Cultivating Self-Control

The following exercise of gathering and concentrating your energy will help you connect to your Inner-G—your inner genius, your inner greatness—while building your self-control. We will repeat this sequence a little later with an added step, as repetition is the key to success.

While you are seated in a comfortable position with your spine straight and your posture erect, do the following:

1. Slowly inhale through the back of your throat for up to five seconds.

2. Draw that breath into your lungs, diaphragm, and belly.

3. Now hold that breath for ten seconds (or as long as you can—the goal is ten).

4. To the count of five, slowly exhale through your mouth all the air in your lungs.

5. Take a big deep inhale and then a long, controlled exhale.

6. Now relax and let your breath return to its normal rhythm.

7. Repeat this exercise two more times while remaining as still and relaxed as you can.

See illustration on next page.

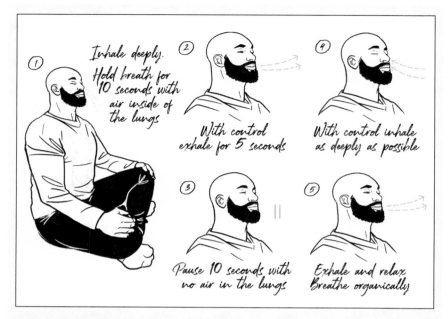

What you gain from this exercise:

- It helps you appreciate life on a deeper level because you become aware of how precious a single breath can be.

- You learn how to control your breath and emotions and not let them control you.

- You discover that no one moment or situation is too big for you. The fear of being overwhelmed dissolves.

THE ZONE

If you just sit and observe, you will see how restless your mind is. If you try to calm it, it only makes things worse. But over time it does calm, and when it does, there's room to hear more subtle things. That's when your intuition starts to blossom and you start to see things more clearly and be in the present more. Your mind just slows down, and . . . you see so much more than you could see before.

—STEVE JOBS

Have you ever had a dream that seemed real? The touch, smell, feel, and excitement of it? And then the following morning, you wake up and know that your dream will crystallize and become a reality? The first time it happened to me, as I described earlier in the book, was when I was five, anticipating the arrival of a new bike. The second time it happened was back in college, and it turned out to be a powerful experience of the zone.

In 2003 I was a sophomore at Georgia Tech and by that time had spent two years as a walk-on. After a series of circumstances that finally did lead to a scholarship, I became the team's starting running back and was about to face one of our biggest opponents of the season, Florida State. It was an away game, and we all knew their home crowd was intimidating and the noise so deafening that it would be hard to hear our own thoughts.

We arrived in Tallahassee on Friday afternoon for the Saturday night game. After an early dinner and team meeting, followed by a chaplain service and inspirational story by Derrick Moore, I was ready to play FSU right then and there! That night, as my room-mate and I slept, we had the Amerie album *All I Have* playing in the background, and I had the dream. In it I ran for a long touchdown, diving into the end zone. I felt and was aware of every step, every movement: the give of the turf, the wind on my face, the taste of sweat, the pursuit of defenders, the elation of crossing the goal line. The scene probably lasted all of a few seconds. The next morning, while lying in bed I felt the warmth of the sun shining through the window and my body was very still while I recalled the vividness of the dream. Suddenly, my eyes popped opened and I whispered out loud, "I'm going to score a touchdown tonight!" At that moment, I knew my dream was going to become a reality.

That night the crowd was electrifying! I was ready for my dream to come true because GT had not beaten FSU in years. During the game I kept trying to make something spectacular happen, but it was a defensive battle into the fourth quarter. I felt physically spent and realized I was applying too much effort, "pushing the river," as some might describe it.

It was late in the game, and I was in the huddle. My quarterback called the play: "44 gut on two. Set. Break!" I remember talking to myself while we were lining up, wondering about my dream from the night before, remembering the dream I had when I was five. I took a deep inhale and held it as I lined up exactly six and a half yards behind the quarterback. I remember saying, "Oh well," letting it all go, and that was when it happened: a simple exhale that released all eagerness, all expectations, all anxiety. My mind became focused, and my spirit became calm. I recalled every con-versation I'd had prior to the game, my preparation the previous week, watching film, working on my stiff-arm, my spin move, my speed, Coach telling us, "These guys put their clothes on just like you. Play with all the confidence in the world!"

"Blue 8! Blue 8! Set. Hut, hut!"

On the second hut, everything around me suddenly slowed down, as if I had entered some other realm. It was the same scene from last night's dream. The quarterback handed me the ball, and I immediately saw FSU linebackers coming toward me. The next thing I knew, I was flowing into a running lane on the left side as if being pulled by gravity. Once I broke through, I again flashed on those conversations about how I should rely on my speed and not stiff-arm so soon "because it slows you down." These thoughts were playing out while I was running from and through defenders! Then I was off to the races down the sideline.

I popped back into reality and realized what was going on. "Oh shit, I'm still running! Feet don't fail me now. Dig, dig, dig!" My foot hit the three-yard line, and I leaped toward the end zone at the same time an FSU defensive back met me in midair. But he was half a second late. When I hit the ground, I couldn't hear a thing at first. I felt as if I had just woken up from a dream. But I quickly realized this was no dream. I had scored the touchdown, and in that moment, my dream and reality had become one.

We lost the game by a point, but my vivid experience of the zone, of being in the flow, which I can still recall in great detail, stayed with me and helped me to understand what I was experiencing years later when I started to seriously practice meditation. It was the same space I felt in my dream, the same space I felt in the game, the same space I rediscovered during my time at the monastery. They all had something in common: an absence of physical or mental resistance. For the aspiring ultimate athlete, there will be a few aches and pains, and getting past the anxieties, desires, and chatter of the mind is tough because it's like a perpetual computer that regulates much of your social, functional, and motor skills. But when you transcend them, what follows is unmistakable. You feel like you're in a large, empty, soundproof room, the only thoughts and sensations your own, no external noise to interfere.

For me it's as if my spirit is on the other side of my everyday reality, patiently waiting for me to figure out the puzzle of how to get past the distractions.

What Is the Zone?

The zone is a state of being in which the awareness of time seems to stop and everything that is happening seems perfectly coordinated, productive, and flowing. There is only the present moment and effortless action. It's a space of enhanced confidence and focus where your entire self is working as a whole. It's more likely to occur when you've connected with your Inner-G, your inner genius, or the unique energy that defines your deepest self. When you've aligned body, mind, and spirit, when you're in touch with who you are and where you want to go, the doors to this deeper part of you open up, and all things are possible.

The zone is another way of describing what has been identified in this area of research as flow. When you're in the zone, you're flowing in harmonious synchronicity. When you flow, you have entered the zone. Either way you look at it, you're performing at the peak of your potential for that particular task. If you intend to become an ultimate athlete, it is the zone that you seek.

University of Chicago professor of psychology Mihaly Csikszentmihalyi *(Me-high Cheek-sent-me-high)* came up with the idea of "flow" in the 1970s after interviewing athletes, musicians, artists, and others about what it felt like when they experienced the peak of their creativity or performance. In *Flow: The Psychology of Optimal Experience* (1990), he described a common feature to all of them:

> *[Flow is] a state in which people are so involved in an activity that nothing else seems to matter; the experience is so enjoyable that people will continue to do it even at great cost, for the sheer sake of doing it. . . . [It] usually occurs if a person's body or mind is stretched to its limits in a voluntary effort to accomplish something different and worthwhile.*

Flow, he says, is characterized by "intense concentration, loss of self-awareness, (and) a feeling of being perfectly challenged."[21]

This last point is really important. No matter what sport you play, no matter what level you're trying to reach, when you're performing at the peak of *your* abilities, the zone is in reach. But you probably won't get there if those abilities are a poor match for the situation. A fencer won't flow if their competition is less skilled; they'll get distracted by boredom. And they will likely get frustrated if their competitor is a lot better. So when it comes to competing with others, it's good to find a comparable group of athletes that can help improve your game.

> **"Flow usually occurs if a person's body or mind is stretched to its limits in a voluntary effort to accomplish something different and worthwhile."**

However, when it comes to training, competing with yourself, it can happen at any time. You just have to raise your body, mind, spirit, emotional intelligence, and energy to a certain level of maturity and awareness. An out-of-shape, undisciplined, distracted "athlete" will never reach the zone. Flip those words around, and you can almost guarantee it. But it's not something you can plan for or predict. There is no ego involved. You just do the work and create the conditions for the zone to appear. We do this unconsciously every day of our lives—we just aren't aware that we're doing it!

That said, the higher you raise the bar for yourself, the more likely you'll enter the zone, because you keep pushing through and beyond your limits. So aim high! Keep going to the outer fringes of the next limit, and then the next limit, and the next. This is how the world's best athletes push themselves to excel and exceed. And when they do:

- Kobe Bryant scores 81 points during a 2006 NBA game.

- Calvin Johnson Jr. sets the NFL record for most receiving yards in a single season (2012)

- Peyton Manning sets the NFL record for game-winning touchdowns.

- Multiple world-record holder Usain Bolt becomes the greatest sprinter of all time.

- Naomi Osaka becomes the first Japanese tennis player to win a Grand Slam.

- Michael Phelps wins eight gold medals at the 2008 Olympics.

- Lindsey Vonn breaks the record for total World Cup victories.

- Tiger Woods wins the 2019 Masters after years of back surgery.

- Snowboarder Shawn White breaks the record for the most X Games and Olympic gold medals.

- Rock climber Alex Honnold free-solos El Capitan in Yosemite.

- Simone Biles becomes the most decorated American gymnast of all time.

- P. J. Daniels (I couldn't resist!) sets an NCAA record for most rushing yards in a bowl game.

You get the picture. But no matter what sport you're in, at whatever level, when you are performing at your optimal potential, when you are reaching or exceeding your personal best, you will experience the same magic that any world-class athlete experiences. The zone is the space where the ultimate athlete produces impossible results and miraculous performances. In the zone no moment goes unnoticed; you are fully immersed and mindful, flowing and aware. There is nothing quite like it. And once you've experienced the zone, it's easy to identify it in others.

Not to be too repetitious, but to summarize what is happening when you are in the zone:

- The mind becomes hyperfocused on a single goal and nothing else.

- Your decision-making is precise, instantaneous, and instinctual.

- Your breathing is steady and synchronized.

- You lose track of time. Every millisecond feels like a minute. There is only the present moment. No energy is wasted worrying about previous mistakes, current possibilities, or future predictability.

- Every cell in your body is humming at peak efficiency.

- Everything around you slows down and feels alive. You are hyperaware of your surroundings but able to concentrate on the task at hand.

The effort feels effortless.

This last point is especially amazing. When you're in the zone, the effort required may not seem like an effort at all. It all just kind of happens. To understand why that is, it's helpful to know what is—and isn't—going on in the brain when one is in the zone.

> In the zone, no moment goes unnoticed; you are fully immersed and mindful, flowing and aware.

Brain Chemistry and the Zone

As we all know, the brain is in constant motion, processing and reacting to every thought and stimulus that enters its awareness. While in the zone, your brain does a much better job of filtering and prioritizing those distractions. It's able to make split-second decisions that you aren't aware of regarding what is and isn't worth paying attention to. Problems seem to resolve themselves automatically. That's why it feels like a flow—everything is happening instantaneously. The brain doesn't keep stopping to react or analyze everything. When you flow in the zone, you aren't thinking, you aren't struggling physically. You don't second-guess. You act instinctively and immediately to what is in front of you without doubt or hesitation—like believing in my speed to outrun those FSU defenders instead of trying to stiff-arm them. It's a much more efficient use of energy that enhances athletic performance.

Now, you might have heard of something called the runner's high. Long-distance runners have frequently reported that they enter a groove where the body starts moving effortlessly and the mind becomes calm and sometimes euphoric even though they've been going for miles. Researchers think it might have something to do with the release of certain neurotransmitters including serotonin, norepinephrine, and endorphins, the last of which kicks in when you've really been pushing it. "Endorphin" comes from the words "endogenous," which means produced in the body, and "morphine," a chemical in opium that elevates mood and reduces pain. Studies of athletes have found that their endorphin levels go up with heavy exercise, helping them get past pain thresholds. This helps to explain why long-distance runners get "high," but anyone who is fit, focused, and pushing their mental and physical limits can trigger such an experience.

The great thing is that the flow state of mind that describes the zone is always available—it doesn't just happen during peak athletic performance. You just have to create the conditions for experiencing it. This is one of the main reasons why meditation is necessary. Meditation is essentially practice for experiencing the zone. Like the zone, it is an altered state of consciousness. When you're truly focused and calm, when those distracting thoughts have subsided, you've entered a flow, a state of timelessness. The more you experience this state, the less effort it takes to return to it.

> Meditation is essentially practice for experiencing the zone. Like the zone, it is an altered state of consciousness.

Predictors of Flow

I mentioned peak athletic performance above, and it's important to understand a bit more about it. The idea has been around for a while. Abraham Maslow, the psychologist who came up with the hierarchy of needs pyramid (starting with basic physical needs at the bottom—the ones you have to satisfy first—and reaching self-actualization at the top), introduced peak performance in the 1960s when trying to describe what people experienced when they felt completely connected and focused. Others have associated peak performance with functional excellence, when you are operating at the highest potential of body, mind and spirit. There's no question for me that when you are in the zone, you are functioning at that high level: physically prepared, mentally sharp, and spiritually connected.

Olympic athletes know how to get to the zone. Physically and mentally, they are at the peak of their abilities. And yet even these premier athletes can falter if they aren't totally locked in. As reported in a 1998 literature review, research done on 160 Olympic athletes found a strong correlation between performance and mental preparedness. [22] Specifically, those who performed the best were described as being

1. mentally ready
2. able to tune out distractions
3. focused
4. visually prepared (they had done extensive visual imagery of what they wanted to achieve)
5. committed to disciplined training and goal-setting

Other studies have shown that the characteristics separating high-performing athletes from lower-performing athletes are a commitment to quality training, daily goal-setting, the regular use of imagery techniques, and a system of mental preparation before they competed.[23] Along with confidence and motivation, these factors also predicted the likelihood of an athlete experiencing a flow state.[23]

The value of imagery and mental preparation links directly back to your breath and the practice of mindfulness and meditation. What better way is there to prepare your mind than sitting quietly, letting go of distracting thoughts, and, while controlling your breath, imagining in detail what you want to achieve and how you will achieve it, such as a golfer perfecting a new swing or a swimmer anchoring a new technique? Research has been done for years on the impacts of using imagery to improve skills, performance, and reaching a flow state. Recent studies on tennis players, for example, showed an increase in flow experiences, improved ball striking, and even a rise in ranking after practicing a series of imagery and contemplative techniques.[24] Soccer players, table tennis players, gymnasts, archers, skaters, and many others can attest to the power of visualization. [25]

Researchers often talk about predictors of flow, and two psychological factors that stand out as influencing one's ability to get into the zone are confidence and anxiety. An attitude of confidence is an invitation to the zone: "You'll see it when you believe it." Confidence was found in many studies to be the most important influence on the ability of an athlete to have a flow experience. Anxiety has the opposite effect; it sabotages athletic performance and reduces one's ability to experience the zone.[26] [27]

> What better way is there to prepare your mind than sitting quietly, letting go of distracting thoughts, and, while controlling your breath, imagining in detail what you want to achieve and how you will achieve it?

One paper in particular that caught my eye was a systematic review of seventeen studies published between 2012 and 2017.[28] It found that the biggest predictors of an experience of flow, of hitting the zone, had to do with psychological factors and personality characteristics such as confidence, being positive, being calm and relaxed, commitment, motivation, attention/focus, and the ability to let go. All of these things are happening inside of our minds, which means we have the ability to control them.

So while you may not be an elite or Olympic athlete (yet!), the practices and qualities that got them to the top are the same as the ones that will take you to your own ultimate achievements. To reach the highest level of their sport, they didn't prepare any differently than anyone who applies the skills and techniques discussed in this book. Optimal functioning and peak performance are within your reach as well.

Meditation and the Zone

In many ways getting to the zone is the culmination of everything I've presented up to this point. When you go into deep meditation, you are priming the body, mind, and spirit to work together, using the techniques of this practice to lock in the body, clear the mind, and access the motivation of the spirit. There's a sense of calm and alertness. There are no distractions. You are focused on the present moment, mindful of everything around you, but not attached. And while sometimes it seems that nothing is happening when you're in this state, the fact that you got there is the point. You've slowed down, cleared your mind, and calmed your body. You've prepared yourself for the zone. In fact, during deep meditation, you're already in the zone. Take some time to breathe and contemplate that.

The zone is simply a different state of awareness. As I've explained, when you're in the zone during training or competition, everything feels different from your usual consciousness. The same thing happens in meditation and when you practice mindfulness, your experience shifts, time disappears, and there is only what is happening in the present moment.

The thing is, the zone is always present. You aren't making it up or creating it if you experience it while meditating or during intense training or competition. It's already there, waiting for you. It's always been there. Think of yourself as a radio adjusting its antenna to find the strongest, clearest signal. When you find it, you've connected with the zone, though you may not necessarily be conscious of that. It can certainly happen without expectation, such as when you are deeply intent on improving your skills and you get into a rhythm. Then *BOOM!* There it is. That rhythm and concentration can take you there.

When you begin your practice of meditation, it can feel like a struggle, like the beginning of training for a new season. Those first two weeks are a grind! But like training, the more you do it, the easier it gets. You start setting the bar higher, training and preparing for a better and stronger performance. You are developing a new skill. At first, you're just trying to learn it and figure out how to apply it and make it work for you. As you learn and advance, the pieces start coming together. It starts to feel more effortless. Your focus deepens. Your confidence grows. Your instincts and intuition kick in, and the new skill becomes a part of you.

As you build your practice, doing it consistently and for longer durations, you start to experience what I call advanced meditation. You're very calm and focused, and time slows down. Your body, mind, and spirit feel completely integrated. Does this sound familiar? Yes, you are now in the zone. How did you get there? With commitment, self-discipline, habit, peace, and focus—the same qualities identified in the research that describe high-performing athletes who get to the zone more often than their competitors. You see the connection? Meditation isn't just a powerful training tool; it's also a tool for concentrating your energy and focus, preparing you for breakthrough experiences. And once you experience the zone in meditation, it becomes easier to get there again, but only with consistent and dedicated practice—just like anything else.

> When you go into deep meditation, you are priming the body, mind, and spirit to work together, using the techniques of this practice to lock in the body, clear the mind, and access the motivation of the spirit.

I can't say this enough. The consistent practice of meditation creates a bridge between your dreams and reality, between what your deeper self aspires to and what you actually manifest. As you go back and forth across this bridge, you begin to experience moments of deep realization, self-awareness, and ultimately self-actualization: the feeling of having reached your highest potential. At this point the two experiences have merged to share the same reality—a *dreality*.

In the zone you will discover ultimate confidence in your body, mind, and spirit. You are acutely aware of your energy and emotions. This is the definition of ultimate—it's the point when you have finally arrived, where everything comes together, back to the core. After coming out of the zone, you feel like you've awakened from a dream. But it's very real, more real than what you experience in day-to-day life. Think about *that* for a moment.

Visualization and the Zone

As I mentioned earlier, the ultimate goal of meditation is highly focused contemplation where you visualize what you want to achieve and experience down to the smallest details. As you do this, you see things that you didn't expect—flaws, areas of resistance, opportunities for improvement—and imagine correcting them. As you visualize your physical and mental conditioning more clearly, these new images and memories become a living part of you, an energetic force that you begin to store like a Jedi knight. Consciously and unconsciously, you are fine-tuning your skill level and improving your game. You start sensing what that feels like throughout your body, even down to a cellular level. As you start to feel it, you start to be it. To accelerate this process, imagine that you have already achieved your goal. Make this a consistent part of your practice. In fact, make reaching your goal a part of your entire being. Find your passion for it, and allow yourself to feel complete confidence that it's real and it will happen.

The zone can happen unexpectedly when training or during competition, but a deep practice of meditation, contemplation, and visualization makes reaching it more likely. By unlocking and aligning the energy and emotions of the body, mind, and spirit, the ultimate athlete connects with higher and higher levels of potential, preparing and positioning them to experience the zone. The more you experience this ability to connect with those higher resonances, the more natural it becomes.

> Learn to control your breathing; don't allow it to control you.

You Have the Tools

Most athletes know there is something inside of them that wants and needs to be expressed, but it's difficult to describe with words. It's easier to show with actions, and the experience of the zone is a confirmation that you have fulfilled that inner yearning. An experience of the zone is a culmination of body, mind, spirit, emotions, and energy coming together in pursuit of a single goal. Each of those areas benefits from meditation and mindfulness in different ways, and all are necessary to break through barriers and overcome limits. More importantly, don't forget your breath, that simple cycle of inhale and exhale. Learn to control your breathing; don't allow it to control you.

If your goal is to become an ultimate athlete and experience the peak of your performance potential, a commitment to meditation will be just as valuable as your commitment to physical training. The road to ultimate, to making the zone the purpose for being alive both in and out of competition, is paved with discipline, dedication, emotional intelligence, and confidence. You know how to get there. Now it's time to do it.

Cultivating Your Inner-G

This is a slightly extended version of the Cultivating Self-Control exercise you did previously, with an added step.

While seated in a comfortable position with your spine straight and your posture erect, do the following:

1. Slowly inhale through the back of your throat for up to five seconds.

2. Draw that breath into your lungs, diaphragm, and belly.

3. Now hold that breath for ten seconds (or as long as you can—the goal is ten).

4. To the count of five, slowly exhale through your mouth all the air in your lungs.

5. At the end of the exhale, pause for another ten seconds. As you count to ten, contract your perineum with each count (located in your pelvic area) as if you are trying to hold a full bladder.

6. Take a deep inhale and then a long, controlled exhale.

7. Now relax and let your breath return to its normal rhythm.

Repeat this exercise two more times while remaining as still and relaxed as you can.

Note: This is a challenging exercise. It takes discipline, focus, and concentration. If you do it correctly, you may initially feel yourself gasping for air, your body temperature will rise, and you will feel the need to inhale before you reach the ten-second goal. Whether or not you reach that goal, your body will experience some discomfort. If this happens, don't panic. Just return to your natural breathing rhythm before trying again. It's not about powering through; it's about maintaining the right technique, staying calm and disciplined as you build your capacity.

With this exercise, you gain a new sense of control, confidence, and awareness and a bridge into the zone.

Visualizing the Ultimate

This visualization exercise complements the one provided earlier but focuses on what you, as an athlete, ultimately aspire to achieve. Here are the steps:

1. Find or create an image that best captures what you want to achieve. This could be a photograph or an image from a magazine or something you create yourself such as a vision board.

2. Stare at this image for at least one minute. Fix the details and the edges of the image in your mind. You may blink a few times, but keep holding your gaze.

3. Now, quickly look at a white or plain wall. An afterimage will emerge, which is the memory of the image that has now engrained itself in your psyche.

4. Your objective is to hold on to that image for as long as you can. After a short time, the image will begin to dissolve.

Now, let's try these same steps with your eyes closed:

1. Use the same image you had above for this exercise.

2. Now, instead of looking at a white wall or surface after staring at the image, close your eyes.

3. Keep your eyes closed as you hold your inner gaze on the afterimage until it disappears.

4. Keep repeating the process, building your focus and concentration until you are able to master retaining the afterimage for at least three minutes.

As you repeat this exercise, you will find over time that your ability to hold the afterimage keeps improving. You are strengthening your ability to turn your dreams and visions into reality.

CONCLUSION
We Are Wired for Greatness

The glory of sport comes from dedication, determination, and desire. Achieving success and personal glory in athletics has less to do with wins and losses than it does with learning how to prepare yourself so that at the end of the day, whether on the track or in the office, you know that there was nothing more you could have done to reach your ultimate goal.
—JACKIE JOYNER-KERSEE

Why did I really write this book? I've always felt a sense of greatness inside myself but never knew how to connect with it until forced to look deep within during a crisis of self-identity. And not just any crisis—I tried to take my own life.

This crisis was the most difficult challenge I've ever had to overcome. More difficult than making it to the NFL after being told "your chances are one in a billion." More difficult than succeeding as a walk-on at Georgia Tech after being told "your chances are one in a million." I survived my planned demise only because I made the choice and took the time to listen, sit still, and be with myself—to meditate.

Fortunately, you don't need to go through a catastrophic event to look within yourself. All you need is your breath and a consistent practice of showing up every day and spending one-on-one time with yourself. It doesn't start out as the easiest thing to do. You have to be able to sit through your own psychological and emotional struggles. Some of these struggles you will already be familiar with, and some will surprise you. But with practice and time, sitting quietly with yourself will become the easiest thing to do, no matter what you may be experiencing. When you can do that, you will have reached the other side, where you find your Inner-G(reatness). This is your true self—no insecurities, no flaws, no fears, no doubts, no mistakes. The authentic you.

And yet meditation is not something you *do*; it's something that you come to understand. When you practice meditation consistently, you *become* more of who you already are. In time you will reach your ultimate self, capable of great feats in your chosen sport as well as in life. This is why I wrote this book: to remind you that nothing is impossible unless you believe it is. On this I speak from experience.

A Blueprint for Breakthrough

On a more practical level, I wanted to teach both aspiring and experienced athletes how to channel and shape their emotions, their energy—their body-mind-spirit—into a high level of maturity that leads to achieving a state called the zone, where you are functioning as a single unit, an integrated whole. To make this happen, though, you have to commit to and believe in your potential. When your mind, heart, and spirit come together in this way, you activate powerful forces in the universe that will support your efforts.

During my time at the monastery, after the trauma of my career-ending football injury, I experienced many powerful moments of personal awareness and personal history. I began to see life more clearly, as well as how all the noise in my head had been keeping me from that knowledge.

When there are no external distractions, the mind starts to look within itself, analyzing

> When you start to diminish that internal chatter, when you mentally disengage from the noise that surrounds you, an amazing thing starts to happen: your mind becomes more functional.

its own thoughts. You come to realize that the mind has always been talking to itself, since you were very young. When you start to diminish that internal chatter, when you mentally disengage from the noise that surrounds you, an amazing thing starts to happen: your mind becomes more functional.

When I was able to spend this quality time with myself, I realized my potential, and that there are no limits other than those I impose. This is no less true for you; you are just as capable of finding your ultimate — it's a natural part of existence.

And so I also wrote this book to emphasize the importance of meditation, of spending quality time with yourself and tapping into the reservoir of your abilities. I'm *not* saying you need to spend time at a monastery. That's extreme! But I am strongly advocating for a consistent practice of looking beyond the five senses for guidance on where you want to go and who you want to be. For me, the sixth sense was my imagination. It gave me access to an innate intelligence I wasn't aware that I had. As we get older, we get stuck navigating the world using only our five senses. The ability to imagine, to go within, to get beyond our labels, becomes more difficult, which makes it all the more important to tap into this power sooner than later. It's the only way I know of to access your ultimate athlete and overcome any limits of your normal thought processes, the ones that keep you from your potential.

Ultimate Is a Process

So now you know the basic components of an ultimate athlete: someone who has harmonized and aligned their body, mind, spirit, emotions, and energy. Someone who believes they can overcome any challenge in front of them with effortless effort, who can flow like water, who has mastered a balance of power and peace.

To put an exclamation point on this, I refer one more time to George Leonard, who introduced the idea of such an individual in his book *The Ultimate Athlete*:

- One who joins body, mind, and spirit in the dance of existence.

- One who explores both inner and outer being.

- One who surpasses limitations and crosses boundaries in the process of personal and social transformation.

- One who plays the larger game, the game of games, with full awareness of the preciousness of life and death and the willingness to accept the pain and joy that come with being truly alive.

- One who serves as a model and guide for others on our collective evolutionary journey.[1]

Becoming an ultimate athlete is not for everyone, although everyone has that innate ability. As you have read in this book, it's a process, a commitment, a life journey that takes discipline and patience. And central to that journey is a practice of mindfulness and meditation. As research has shown, and as countless successful athletes can attest, the benefits to body, mind, and spirit from a dedicated practice are many. Those benefits are cumulative, but they only happen when you commit. With discipline, patience, and consistency, they *will* happen, and they will help take you where you want to go.

Patience and Practice

The key to success is to make your meditation practice a habit. Don't expect to see large gains when you only meditate every now and then. One day a week, for example, gives you a one-in-seven probability of success—not very high. You wouldn't work the body one day a week and expect to see results. So to experience optimal gains from your meditation practice, do it every day for a month and see how you feel. If that's too difficult, try just three times per week. The important thing is to maintain a regimen that is sustainable and consistent, just as you do when in physical training.

Start with one to five minutes a day. Simply sit down in a comfortable place and practice the routines that I've shared in this book. The goal is to be consistent. Meditate in the morning when you wake up, before or after a practice or game, or at night before you sleep. Once a day is all you need. The more you do it, the sooner you will start to notice a difference in your thoughts and emotions and see improvements in your training and performance.

With practice you may see a change in as little as two weeks. After a month you will have created a new habit that will become a major part of your daily life. If you doubt its impacts and want to get a better sense of the benefits of meditation, take a week off after you've created the habit and see what happens. Pay close attention to how you think, feel, and react. You may be quite surprised.

You don't have to do this, of course, but it might help you understand some of the subtle (and not-so-subtle) benefits of a regular practice. I learned this from having done my own testing, which proved that my personal and competitive life flowed more smoothly when I was consistently meditating. I realized that meditation helped me to perceive my life and the world around me differently. Everything felt fresh and new, with more potential—the same thing that happens when you travel to a new country. Think of meditation as an act of internal engineering that will change you for the better from the inside out.

Let It Come to You

As you train, compete, and build your skills using mindfulness and meditation as part of your routine, don't pay too much attention to results. Even if you experience the zone, the secret to raising a bar and then exceeding it is to not overfocus. Don't expect, pray for, obsess on, or hope that breakthrough experiences will happen. Establish a rock-solid routine of practice, and allow the universe to do its magic. It's like breathing. You don't force yourself to breathe; it happens automatically and organically.

If you experience a setback, or improvements don't come as quickly as you'd like, don't get caught up in frustration. Take a deep breath and refocus. Use the skills you've been learning

> Accept an obstacle for what it is, show gratitude for the chance to resolve it, and move on to the next moment.

to get past those negative emotions. Accept an obstacle for what it is, show gratitude for the chance to resolve it, and move on to the next moment. Feelings of gratitude help difficult moments pass gracefully, like enjoying a breath of fresh air. They unleash the potential for resolution. Remember, if you're never challenged, you will never learn. And usually what you learn brings you closer to achieving your goal.

The same lesson applies once you've elevated your game: Continue resisting any obsession with results. If they become your sole objective, you've missed the point of being an ultimate athlete. As my spiritual teacher says, "Do the work for the work's sake." Looking for results is like looking for success without understanding preparation. Don't be desperate or hold on too tightly to what you've achieved. You will maintain it in the same way you achieved it: with patience, relaxation, persistence, dedication, letting go, consistency, and breath.

The other thing about being an ultimate athlete is that it's not an attitude you can simply turn off when you leave the game—nor would you want to. The disciplines and routines you develop while training and competing stay with you when you retire from your sport. These polished skills have become habitual; you can translate and transfer them to a new life, beyond your respective sport. No matter what profession you choose, whether it's business or sports or law or education, the energy of those skills will follow you. Remember, we are all athletes in the game of life. Ultimate doesn't just work at the arena, in the water, or on the track; it becomes part of who you are wherever you go, which will make the job of life that much easier and more meaningful.

As Within, So Without

As I mentioned at the beginning of this chapter, I've always seen something in myself that so fascinated me I wanted to share it with others. Then I realized that I'm no different from you. I learned to use my imagination and mind power to turn my dreams, thoughts, and ideas into reality, and so can you. This is what I really want to share. Most of us perform far below our capacity. If we were able to exercise and activate more of our mind muscle, we would discover that nothing is impossible unless we truly believe it is.

I'm talking about the awesome power of the mind and the spirit, an ability and a gift that goes far beyond the surface levels of how we think about reality. Some of the world's most influential figures came to the same conclusion about how thoughts and our reality are directly connected. For example,

Earl Nightingale:	*"You become what you think about."*
Bruce Lee:	*"As you think, so shall you become."*
Gandhi:	*"A man is but the product of his thoughts. What he thinks, he becomes."*
Buddha:	*"The mind is everything. What you think, you become."*
Ralph Waldo Emerson:	*"You become what you think about all day long."*
Wayne Dyer:	*"As you think, so shall you be."*
English proverb	*"As you sow, so shall you reap."*

The ultimate purpose of a mindfulness and meditation practice is to discover one's inner self, the core being of who you are. This self, this core being, is with you every day of life and during everything you do. It's what makes you truly unique. It's what defines your purpose and mission. It connects you to a higher power, however you define or experience that. The extent to which you can express the fullness of it will make your life as an athlete and as a human being that much more meaningful.

So celebrate what you do and the hard work you put into perfecting your craft. Go and live out what you have imagined, visualized, and aspired to. Play the game you love with passion and joy so that your love becomes the game of life. And don't forget the most important thing: Breathe and have fun!

ENDNOTES

1 George Leonard, *The Ultimate Athlete: Re-visioning Sports, Physical Education and the Body* (Berkeley, CA: North Atlantic Books, 1990), 11.

2 Kate Rope, "The Future of Being Present." *Time: The New Mindfulness*, November 28, 2018.Osho, "Meditation Is a Very Simple Phenomenon," YouTube video, 6:52, uploaded September 28, 2009, https://www.youtube.com/watch?v=0peVQTdI3Yg.

3 Osho, "Meditation Is a Very Simple Phenomenon," YouTube video, 6:52, uploaded September 28, 2009, https://www.youtube.com/watch?v=0peVQTdI3Yg.

4 Christopher Heckman, "The Effect of Mindfulness and Meditation in Sports Performance," *Kinesiology, Sport Studies, and Physical Education Synthesis Projects* (2018): 47.

5 Matthew A. Killingsworth and Daniel T. Gilbert, "A Wandering Mind Is an Unhappy Mind," *Science*, November 12, 2010, 932.

6 Lisa Esposito, "Athletes Can Thrive on Plant-Based Diets," *U.S. News and World Report*, January 11, 2019.

7 Kristian Winfield, "Andre Iguodala's Balancing Act Is on His Dinner Plate, Not the Basketball Court," SBNation.com, November 24, 2017.

8 Enette Larson-Meyer, "Vegetarian and Vegan Diets for Athletic Training and Performance," Gatorade Sports Science Institute, December 2018, gssiweb.org.

9 Carl Zimmer, "The Brain: Why Athletes Are Geniuses," *Discover*, April 2010.

10 Claudio del Percio et al., "'Neural Efficiency' of Athletes' Brain for Upright Standing: A High-Resolution EEG Study," *Brain Research Bulletin* 79, nos. 3–4 (2009): 193–200.

11 S. M. Marcoa et al., "Mental Fatigue Impairs Physical Performance in Humans," *Journal of Applied Physiology* 106, no. 3 (Mar 2009): 857–864.

12 E. Luders et al., "The Unique Brain Anatomy of Meditation Practitioners: Alterations in Cortical Gyrification," *Frontiers in Human Neuroscience* 6 (February 29, 2012): 34.

13 J. A. Grant et al., "Cortical Thickness and Pain Sensitivity in Zen Meditators," *Emotion* 1 (February 2010): 43–53.

14 G. Desbordes et al., "Effects of Mindful-Attention and Compassion Meditation Training on Amygdala Response to Emotional Stimuli in an Ordinary Non-meditative State," *Frontiers in Human Neuroscience* 6 (November 1, 2012): 292.

15 Rod Meade Sperry, ed., *A Beginner's Guide to Meditation* (Boulder, CO: Shambhala Publications, 2014).

16 Joel Pearson, "The Human Imagination: The Cognitive Neuroscience of Visual Mental Imagery," *Nature Reviews: Neuroscience 20* (2019): 624–634.

17 Rollin McCraty, "The Science of HeartMath," HeartMath.com (undated).

18 Rollin McCraty, *The Science of the Heart, Vol. 2: Exploring the Role of the Heart in Human Performance* (Boulder Creek, CA: HeartMath, 2015).

19 Yamada Jirokichi, Kashima Shinden Jikishinkage-ryū 鹿島神傳直心影流 (Tokyo: Suishinsha, 1927).

20 Quoted in Wm. Theodore de Bary, ed., *Sources of Japanese Tradition, Abridged: Part 1: 1600 to 1868*. Introduction to Asian Civilizations (New York: Columbia University Press, 2010), 555.

21 Mihaly Csikszentmihalyi, *Flow: The Psychology of Optimal Experience* (New York: Harper and Row, 1990).

22 Greg Wells, "Peak Performance: A Literature Review," ResearchGate.com, December 1998.

23 Susan A. Jackson, "Factors Influencing the Occurrence of Flow State in Elite Athletes," *Journal of Applied Sport Psychology* 7, no. 2 (1995): 138–166.

24 Stefan Koehn et al., "Imagery Intervention to Increase Flow State and Performance in Competition," *Sports Psychologist* 29, no. 1 (March 2014): 48–59.

25 K. J. Munroe-Chandler and Michelle D. Guerrero, "Psychological Imagery in Sport and Performance," *Sports Psychology* (April 2017). Viewed online at oxfordre.com/psychology.

26 Stefan Koehn et al., "Correlates of Dispositional and State Flow in Tennis Competition," *Journal of Applied Sport Psychology* 25, no. 3 (2013): 354–369.

27 Stefan Koehn, "Effects of Confidence and Anxiety on Flow State in Competition," *European Journal of Sport Science* 13, no. 5 (2013): 543–550.

28 Fotein Stamatelopoulou et al., "Being in the Zone: A Systematic Review on the Relationship of Psychological Correlates and the Occurrence of Flow Experiences in Sports' Performance," *Psychology* 9, no. 8 (2018): 2011–2030.

ACKNOWLEDGMENTS

JoAnn & Steven Randolph, Chanitha Keys, Leybelis, ZoAya and Xaria, Manjah Fernandez, Doug Harrison, Mitch Thrower, Kristen Wright-Matthews, Robert Nsiah, Mike Sager, Liza Biggers, Siori Kitajima, Mama Lessie, Curtis Bernard Keys, Kent Keys, Coach Curtis Modkins, Coach Dogan, Coach Paul Delesbore, Coach Bill Baron, Coach Chan Gailey, Coach Paige, Brad Honeycutt, Kyle Wallace, Nathaniel Dorsey, Jeremy Philips, Leon Robinson, Salih Besirevic, Andy Tidwell-Neal, Garren Findlay, Kevin Tuminello, Derrick Moore, Coach Todd, Steve McNair, Coach Tony Nathan, Coach Wilbert Montgomery, Bart Scott, Jason Carter, Tom Bender, James Cooper, Wilton and Clifton Morgan, DeMarius Bilbo, Darius (DA) Williams, Keyaron Fox, Mario West, Cory Ross, Michael Anderson, Brian Billick, Rev. Kadeem Nazirmoreh (ABRD), Jeff Friday, Matthew Gilbert, Suresh Madhavan, Ted Adams, Prince Ahadzie Daniels Sr., Enisio Sayeh, Mikey Sayeh, Timothy Keys, Julius Keys, Gerris Wilkinson, Marilen Tran, Christopher Lee Kamimura, my family in Ghana, and last but not least Bill O'Brien.

Thank you for being a part of this.

ABOUT THE AUTHOR

Prince "P. J." Daniels Jr. is a storyteller and practitioner of mindfulness and meditation. His life has been spent understanding, practicing, and teaching the benefits of balancing one's power and peace. Daniels's personal story is one of overcoming challenges and determination and commitment to excellence.

His career started as a walk-on, where he earned a scholarship to Georgia Tech after the 2002 season. He then went on to become a two-time all-conference tailback and the fourth leading rusher in Georgia Tech football history, with 3,300 yards. A two-time Academic All-ACC selection, Daniels played in the 2004 Humanitarian Bowl, where he ran for an unbroken NCAA bowl game record of 311 yards and four touchdowns. He was drafted by the NFL's Baltimore Ravens in 2006. His career ended prematurely as a result of injuries in 2009.

After this life-altering experience, Daniels was led to a monastic life centered on meditation. The truth that he uncovered during his time at the monastery changed his life course and led him to help others to uncover the universal truths available to all through contemplation. He encourages people to practice mindfulness and meditation as a means of confronting their fears, pursuing their dreams, finding their balance of power and peace, and enhancing their overall well-being.